Advising the Ultra-Wealthy

Gregory Curtis

Advising the Ultra-Wealthy

A Guide for Practitioners

Gregory Curtis
Greycourt & Co., Inc.
Pittsburgh, PA, USA

ISBN 978-3-030-57604-2   ISBN 978-3-030-57605-9   (eBook)
https://doi.org/10.1007/978-3-030-57605-9

Cover credit image: MP_P

This Palgrave Macmillan imprint is published by the registered company Springer Nature Switzerland AG.
The registered company address is: Gewerbestrasse 11, 6330 Cham, Switzerland

Preface

After serving for many years as head of a family office for "America's Richest Family,"[1] I launched Greycourt & Co., Inc. That was back in 1986, and at the time Greycourt was one of the first independent firms working with ultra-wealthy families. Today, Greycourt continues to be among a small handful of premier independent firms in the ultra-high net worth space, advising ultra-wealthy families in the US, Canada, Latin America, and Europe.

Over the nearly 35 years since Greycourt's founding, I have learned a very great deal about what is required to launch and build a firm serving ultra-wealthy families and to survive and prosper in what is an intensely competitive field. The point of this book is to pass that learning along to other advisors who may be interested in working with the ultra-wealthy.

Every year I talk with many financial advisors who have been successful working with "smaller" families, typically "mass affluent" families with perhaps one or two clients in the $20 million or so range. And, indeed, for advisors who wish to work with very wealthy families, the first requirement is to have demonstrated success working with less wealthy families. After all, most of the core competencies required to be successful with the ultra-wealthy are also required to be successful with a client of any size. See Chap. 1—"Ultra-Wealthy Families and Their Financial Advisors."

Families that own businesses, even very successful ones, often have very little liquidity. Hence, it will be mainly post-liquidity-event families that will be looking for advisors. It has been our experience that the *way* families get rich very directly affects how their accounts should be handled by their

---

[1] David E. Koskoff, *The Mellons: The Chronicle of America's Richest Family*, New York: Thomas Y. Crowell Company, 1978.

advisor. I discuss this phenomenon in Chap. 2—"How Families get Rich (and Why It Matters to You)."

One issue I often encounter is advisors who have worked with mass affluent families but who also have a few larger clients that are institutional in nature. Usually these are foundations, nonprofit organizations with significant endowments, or a college. I have worked extensively with endowed institutions, both as clients and via serving on boards and investment committees. (Indeed, I have served on more than 30 investment committees, chairing most of them.) I believe that wealthy families and institutions are extremely different from each other, even when their asset bases are similar. I discuss these differences in Chap. 3—"Differences Between Wealthy Families and Institutions."

For many advisors, the biggest challenge will be how to attract ultra-wealthy family clients in the first place. It can seem to be an insurmountable hurdle, but in fact, there are tried-and-true techniques that have worked for us over the years and that will also work for you. I discuss those techniques in Chap. 4—"Building an Ultra-Wealthy Family Client Base."

One constant I find in working with ultra-wealthy families is the extreme level of complexity they present. For advisors who are used to working with smaller families, this complexity can come as something of a shock—worse, it can destroy the profitability of the engagement. In many of the following chapters, I discuss some of these complexities, although of course complex issues arise throughout the relationship.

Broadly speaking, the advisory skills required to advise the ultra-wealthy are similar to those required to advise any client: establishing appropriate risk parameters, designing the right portfolio for the family, selecting money managers, and reporting on investment performance. But in every case the specific details of how those activities are carried out will be different—sometimes very significantly different. Much of this book is devoted to outlining those differences.

In "smaller" families, decision-making is usually straightforward—the client (and perhaps his or her spouse) make the decisions. But in wealthy families decision-making can become very complicated very quickly. For example, there may be two, or even three, generations involved in making investment decisions, there may be collateral family units involved (cousins, for example), and there may be a family investment committee that operates on a fiduciary or advisory basis. These issues are discussed in Chap. 8—"On Governance: Decision-Making in Families."

While smaller families will make charitable contributions, for ultra-wealthy families philanthropy will often be a core activity—perhaps the central activity of the family. Philanthropy can be carried out through individual gift-ing (especially the gifting of appreciated securities), through family founda-tions, or through donor-advised funds. I discuss philanthropy in Chap. 9—"Family Philanthropy."

Sometimes an especially thoughtful family will engage an advisor in advance of a liquidity event—a very important step, as it helps ensure that the family will be prepared for the new world of liquid capital they will soon inhabit. There are a few important steps a family should be taking in advance of the sale of their company, and you, as the new advisor, can help guide the family through these steps. See Chap. 10—"They're Selling the Family Company: Now What?"

Perhaps the most important chapter in this book is one of the shortest: Chap. 11—"What Is the Wealth For?" Families that have stayed together and lived happy and productive lives while they ran a family business can find themselves at sea when the business has been sold. It's impossible for family members to identify with something as inconcrete as liquid capital. So what is it that will now hold the family together? It's critically important for families to address the issue of what their wealth is for, and to address it together, as a family.

If this book had been written a decade ago, I probably wouldn't even have mentioned socially responsible investing (SRI). But today SRI plays a central role in family investing, especially for women and Nextgen family members. I deal with SRI in Chap. 12—"Socially Responsible Investing."

Most families who have enough investment assets to require an advisor will also have an estate plan. But for "smaller" families those estate plans will be quite similar and relatively straightforward. It's a very different picture in ultra-wealthy families, where the family may have many trusts (it's not uncom-mon for a very wealthy family to have several hundred family trusts). In addi-tion, wealthy families will typically be taking advantage of a large variety of tax-oriented strategies—GRATs, CRUTs, asset protection trusts, dynasty trusts, and so on. See Chap. 13—"Trusts and Estate Planning."

As everyone in the wealth advisory business knows, families typi-cally devolves from shirtsleeves-to-shirtsleeves in three generations. The break-down of family wealth can certainly happen as a result of poor investment decisions, but more often, it results from family breakdown itself. Families whose wealth survives beyond the third generation do so by paying every bit as much attention to human capital as they do to financial capital. I discuss family coherence in Chap. 15, under the section titled "Nextgen and Family Transitions."

Since this book is addressed to financial advisors who are already skilled at many things, rather than go into excruciating detail about issues you are already familiar with, I have simply lumped into one chapter a variety of matters you already understand but which may have to be beefed up to succeed in the world of the ultra-wealthy. I include brief sections on asset allocation, recurring mistakes wealthy families make, Nextgen issues and family transitions, portfolio reporting systems, and goals and objectives. See Chap. 14—"Strengthening Your Existing Knowledge."

In the last chapter I discuss several issues you will encounter advising wealthy families that are absent in smaller families. For example, smaller investors will typically use mutual funds, index funds, or ETFs, while wealthier families will more commonly use separately managed accounts. In the latter case, an asset custodian will need to be engaged.

While all families pay taxes, taxes are a huge issue for ultra-wealthy families. Taxes must be considered from the very beginning, when designing the portfolio; they must be taken into account when selecting managers; and, finally, tax issues are usually central when selling positions (paying attention to long-term gains and to offsetting losses against gains).

Smaller families don't have family offices, but most ultra-wealthy families do. As an advisor, you will often interface more frequently with family office personnel than with family members themselves.

Finally, you may wish to update your standard-form advisory agreement before you begin to work with ultra-wealthy families.

Pittsburgh, PA   Gregory Curtis

Contents

List of Tables

Introduction

The Ultra-Wealthy Family and You

Scott Fitzgerald supposedly once remarked to Ernest Hemingway, "Let me tell you about the very rich. They are different from you and me."

Whether or not the rich are different, rich *investors* are certainly different. The level of complexity of their investment portfolios can be mind-boggling to the uninitiated. On the other hand, the investment fundamentals that apply to smaller investors apply with equal force to the ultra-wealthy—it's just that the numbers are vastly larger and, therefore, the consequences of mistakes can be bone-chilling.

Still, no one starts out life being ready to serve as a financial advisor to extremely complex, ultra-wealthy families. Yet, those of us who are in the wealth advisory business all got there somehow, and so can you.

In this book, I have assumed that my readers are already accomplished financial professionals experienced in working with smaller clients, but that those readers are interested in competing for much larger mandates. Thus, most of the material that would appear in a normal investment book has been left out. What I focus on in these pages are the *differences* involved in advising the ultra-wealthy.

I've worked with ultra-wealthy families for nearly half a century, initially as legal counsel and then, for the past 40 years, as a financial advisor. I worked for one of the world's largest law firms, Reed Smith, in the mid-1970s and then managed a family office for members of the Mellon family for 15 years. I then formed Greycourt & Co., Inc., which remains one of the world's premier wealth management firms.

The World of Ultra-Wealthy Families

How many ultra-wealthy families are there in the US? The short answer is, "No one knows." According to the Boston Consulting Group (BCG), there are more than 5000 US households worth $100 million or more, but that is an estimate. The total could easily be twice that high. Globally, BCG projects that ultra-wealthy families now control about $18 trillion. UBS and PwC estimate that wealth in the U.S. controlled by billionaires totaled $10.2 trillion in 2020.

Estimates of how many family offices exist are also soft, ranging from 3000 to 10,000 offices in the US, with many more on a global basis. On one issue, though, there is wide agreement—this sector of the market is growing very rapidly.

Organization of the Book

Chapter 1—"Ultra-Wealthy Families and Their Financial Advisors"
I describe the population of ultra-wealthy families and the challenges they face in their struggle to remain wealthy. I then outline the human and technical skills required to advise these families.

Chapter 2—"How Families Get Rich (and Why It Matters to You)"
I describe the various ways families become wealthy and why those differing paths matter to you as their future financial advisor. Advisors who work with wealthy families will find that there is usually a very large difference between working with the wealth creator—the entrepreneur—and working with subsequent generations. I discuss some of those differences and how advisors can best navigate this complex world.

Chapter 3—"Differences Between Wealthy Families and Institutions"
Many financial advisors who have not yet worked extensively with ultra-wealthy families actually do have experience working with rather large endowed institutions. In this chapter I emphasize the important distinctions between families and institutions, distinctions that directly affect how you will approach the challenge of advising wealthy families.

Chapter 4—"Building an Ultra-Wealthy Family Client Base"
It may seem daunting to find that first ultra-wealthy client and then to build a successful wealth advisory business. But there are tried-and-true methods for accomplishing these things.

Chapter 5—"A Wealthy Family's Many Advisors"

The world of advisors to wealthy families is a vast and complex one, but it is an area that needs to be understood by financial advisors who wish to work with those families. Financial advisors will need to interface with, coordinate and cooperate with, and adjust their advice in light of the work that is being done for families by legal (especially estate and trust planning) advisors, tax advisors (who may be accountants or attorneys), philanthropic advisors, family dynamics advisors, and many others.

Chapter 6—"Policy Statements for Wealthy Families"

Given the complexity of an ultra-wealthy family's financial affairs, carefully written policy statements are crucial. In this chapter, I supply samples of various policy statements most families will need.

Chapter 7—"Evaluating Money Managers for Family Portfolios"

Some of the issues associated with evaluating money managers are common regardless of the nature of the investor. However, for advisors working with wealthy families, additional issues will need to be considered. These include the tax efficiency of the manager's investment activities, the liquidity of the investment, the willingness of the manager to incorporate a family's specific tax needs (by trading specific tax lots, for example), and similar matters.

Chapter 8—"On Governance: Decision-Making in Families"

Most wealthy families begin their lives as investors with one or two decision makers who make all the judgments. These are typically the wealth creator and his or her spouse. But as younger generations come of age, family governance becomes more complex. I discuss some of the key issues associated with family governance and suggest ways of dealing with them.

Chapter 9—"Family Philanthropy"

In most wealthy families, philanthropic issues will be handled either inside the family or with an outside philanthropic advisor. Nonetheless, advisors need to understand how philanthropic vehicles work and the importance of philanthropy to most wealthy families.

Chapter 10—"They're Selling the Family Company: Now What?"

I suggest a list of ten key steps a family should think through—with your help—and implement when they are about to sell the family company.

Chapter 11—"What Is the Wealth For?"

Whether an advisor is working for the wealth creator or with subsequent generations, the core question for the family is, "What is our wealth for?" Families—and individual family members—will answer this question in different ways, but advisors need to be aware of how important the question is and should be ready to assist family members in answering it.

Chapter 12—"Socially Responsible Investing"

While SRI has been around for decades, its prominence has increased greatly in recent years. Although some SRI investors are prepared to sacrifice returns in pursuit of their ethical goals, I will also suggest approaches that consider these issues without sacrificing returns and will cite academic evidence for which social/ESG/sustainable factors matter to returns and which don't.

Chapter 13—"Trusts and Estate Planning"

A full treatment of this topic is far beyond the purview of this book. In this chapter, I focus on the *investment* implications of common tax and estate planning techniques.

Chapter 14—"Strengthening Your Existing Knowledge"

As a skilled financial advisor, you don't need me to tell you how to advise clients. But to work successfully with the ultra-wealthy, you may need to strengthen your existing skills. In this chapter, I include brief sections on asset allocation, recurring mistakes wealthy families make, Nextgen issues and family transitions, portfolio reporting systems, and goals and objectives.

Chapter 15—"Miscellaneous Issues that Affect the Ultra-Wealthy"

In this chapter, I briefly discuss asset custody, managing investment taxes, working with family offices, and rethinking your standard advisory agreement.

I hope you find this book useful and wish you well in your quest to work with America's—and the world's—ultra-wealthy families.

1

Ultra-Wealthy Families and Their Financial Advisors

Reporter, buttonholing an oil tycoon: *Sir, are you aware that your son just lost one million dollars on a sports franchise?*

Tycoon: *At that rate the boy'll be broke in 315 years!*

No, a family doesn't have to have $315 million to be considered ultra-wealthy, though it certainly helps. In reality, being ultra-wealthy is more a state of mind than an amount of money. A family that takes its wealth seriously—one that focuses on the stewardship of that wealth for future generations, that thinks *dynastically*—is far more likely to be, and continue to be, ultra-wealthy.

On the other hand, no matter how much money a family controls, if that family treats its wealth frivolously, if it over-spends and under-invests, if it ignores its own human capital, that family won't be wealthy for long: shirtsleeves-to-shirtsleeves in three generations has been, and always will be, the norm for most families.

All that said, an ultra-wealthy family needs to control a certain minimum amount of capital. There is no absolute cut-off or minimum, but it's useful to note that most of the better wealth advisory firms have minimum account sizes of $50 million to $100 million. (Or at least minimum account fees that back into accounts of that size.) Some families with less capital than that will still be ultra-wealthy-like, but most won't be.

To put these numbers in perspective, note that the average American family has a net worth of about $700,000, and most of that (north of 70%) is tied up in their homes. And the *median* net worth is far smaller—less than $100,000. Obviously, ordinary Americans don't have much liquid capital to

© The Author(s) 2020

G. Curtis, *Advising the Ultra-Wealthy*, https://doi.org/10.1007/978-3-030-57605-9_1

invest, and what they do have is likely to be in a retirement account—IRAs and 401(k) plans, for example.

Wealth is very unevenly distributed in most countries, and the US is no exception. According to an analysis by the University of California at Santa Cruz,[1] the top 1% of families own 35% of all wealth and the next 19% control an additional 50%. On the other hand, when people refer to "the top 1%," they aren't referring to what I am discussing in this book. To be in the top 1% in terms of wealth requires a net worth of only about $5 million. In other words, the ultra-wealthy are—at least!—the top 1% of the top 1%.

As families climb up the net worth spectrum, they begin to resemble the ultra-wealthy, albeit with less complexity, especially regarding family office issues. Still, the main point is that while advising an ultra-wealthy family is nothing like advising a mass affluent family (people with @ $2 million–$5 million in investable assets), it is really a spectrum. By the time advisors are working with families with $25 million, even if it's only a few clients, they are dealing with issues quite similar to those faced by the true ultra-wealthy.

For purposes of this book, I consider the ultra-wealthy to begin at the $50 million level and preferably higher—many of the best wealth advisory firms enforce a $100 million minimum account size. But of course, there are exceptions. Consider a family with $40 million of liquid capital but which controls a business worth $300 million. Such a family will still operate under the same *investment* constraints as families with $25 million or less, but they will also have the resources to behave, in most ways, like a true ultra-wealthy family.

Such a family will likely have established a family office—perhaps with some of the company executives playing dual roles at the company and the family office. The family will need to take seriously such issues as succession planning (since that will affect the company as well as the family), human capital, family dynamics, and so on. This family's investment portfolio might look a lot like that of a smaller family's, but they are truly in the ultra-wealthy category.

What Does It Take to Remain Ultra-Wealthy?

Remaining wealthy—to say nothing of *ultra*-wealthy—requires a family to succeed on many fronts. That's why so many families fail. Here, in roughly their order of importance, are the main challenges the ultra-wealthy face:

---

[1] G. William Domhoff, *Wealth, Income, and Power,* http://www1bpt.bridgeport.edu/-jconlin/EssayDomhoffWealthIncomePower.pdf

- Maintaining and, if possible, improving, the family's human capital.
- Controlling spending.
- Learning to govern the family wisely.
- Planning for succession in family leadership.
- Educating younger family members in the obligations and skills of stewardship.
- Putting in writing all the key family policies: spending, governance, succession, investment, and so on.
- Employing only best-in-class advisors across the board.
- Developing an investment strategy that is appropriately designed to meet the family's risk tolerance and investment objectives on an after-tax basis— *regardless of how different that strategy might be from the strategies pursued by others.*
- Optimizing investment fees as well as fees paid to other advisors.
- Investing with only the best investment managers and funds available, and avoiding high-cost proprietary products.

In the chapters that follow, I will address each of these challenges, as well as others, and will suggest best practices that, if followed by advisors and the families they work with, will stack the odds in favor of remaining in the ultra-wealthy category while most others fall by the wayside.

What Human Skills Are Required to Advise the Ultra-Wealthy?

I often hear it said that a successful wealth advisor must be both a first-rate investment professional and also a talented psychiatrist. That is an exaggeration—the ultra-rich are perfectly capable of finding their own therapists—but there is a kernel of truth to it. Wealth advisors don't need to be psychiatrists, but they do need to be good *listeners*.

Of course, all good advisors listen carefully to their clients before making recommendations, but the level of complexity of ultra-wealthy families requires a whole new level of listening. For example, I have sometimes worked with families *for more than a year* before making any major changes in their portfolios or practices.

As I noted above, a key challenge for every ultra-wealthy family is:

Developing an investment strategy that is appropriately designed to meet the family's risk tolerance and investment objectives on an after-tax basis—*regardless of how different that strategy might be from the strategies pursued by others.*

But how does an advisor know what the family's tolerance for risk is? How does the *family* know what its risk tolerance is? And the same two questions can be asked about the family's investment objectives. The only way to understand these kinds of issues is to talk with the family about them—often at great length and over extended periods of time.

Indeed, there are far more *wrong* ways to advise the ultra-rich than there are right ways. Here are just a few of them:

- Not listening.
- Putting a family's money to work in the capital markets too quickly, before both the advisor and the family fully understand what they are doing and why.
- Working in an advisory business model that *encourages* capital to be put to work too quickly. That is, if an advisor can't get paid until the money is invested, that advisor will be sorely tempted to do the wrong thing.

In addition to being a good listener, successful wealth advisors need to be *diplomats*. Families sometimes need to hear hard things—that they are overspending, for example, or are reacting to short-term market events. These aren't easy matters to hear or deal with, but advisors who can raise such issues diplomatically will have much greater success convincing their clients to do the right thing.

Wealth advisors need to maintain a calm and confident *demeanor* (though never approaching arrogance), especially during difficult market environments. If the stock market is crashing and the advisor seems skittish or agitated, the family is likely to be spooked.

Wealth advisors need to be fundamentally *humble*. The simple fact is that no one knows what the markets are going to do and everyone is going to get it wrong occasionally. Advisors must acknowledge the unknowability of the markets while still positioning the family to weather the most likely scenarios.

And—this is crucial—wealth advisors must *admit their mistakes*. It's never easy to acknowledge that we were wrong and that our advice cost the family money. But being honest about failed strategies will almost always build confidence rather than destroy it.

When a family has become ultra-wealthy, that family has, by definition, been incredibly successful. Family members are likely to be extremely astute and to exercise exceptionally good judgment about matters in general.

However, almost no families became wealthy through managing broadly diversified portfolios (Warren Buffet might be an exception, depending on how we define "diversified").

Therefore, wealth advisors are faced with the constant challenge of working with successful, confident, capable people who, nonetheless, know very little about managing liquid wealth. Balancing respect for what the family has accomplished with the understanding that the families are navigating very new waters, is a difficult role to play, but it is an essential one.

What Technical Skills Are Required to Advise the Ultra-Wealthy?

A good part of this book is dedicated to the development of the technical skills required to successfully design and manage large, taxable investment portfolios. But let's start by observing that while many of the technical skills required for wealth advisors are similar to the skills required to be successful in allied professions (money management, for example, hedge fund management, or even stockbrokering), those skills will be deployed in a very different context.

I once served on an investment committee for a university with one of the world's great money managers, and I looked forward to hearing his insights into the market and into how the endowment should be positioned. To my surprise, the money manager proved to be an unconstructive member of the committee.

Why? Because money managers are engaged in a different activity, one that has very different risk and reward characteristics and very different consequences. This money manager had interesting opinions about obscure sectors of the market (German bunds, Italian real estate), but these were of no practical use to the endowment.

In addition, the money manager had a very different idea about risk, namely, that a few disastrous trades or even a few very bad years of performance would be forgiven by his investors because of his long and successful track record.

But the endowment didn't exist for the personal benefit of the money manager—it had to serve the interests of thousands of students, faculty and alumni, none of whom had much patience for extremely poor performance.

To use an analogy, the money manager was like an extremely agile speedboat, while the endowment was like a massive aircraft carrier. The speedboat could maneuver quickly in any direction and often recover from trouble due simply to its nimbleness. The endowment moved very slowly, was unable to engage in lightening trades or to recover quickly if matters went awry.

Here are some of the technical skills advisors need to master if they expect to work with the ultra-rich:

- Advisors need to understand the liability side of a family's balance sheet, especially spending and fixed and contingent liabilities.
- Asset allocation is a complex subject, especially for taxable investment portfolios that are expected to remain invested for generations. But a family's strategic allocation will be the primary driver of its risk and return, so advisors need to master the subject thoroughly.
- The world and its capital markets don't stand still, and as a result advisors to the ultra-wealthy need to alertly make tactical adjustments to the family's portfolio, moving away from areas of high risk and toward areas of special reward. On the other hand, since changes in family portfolios typically result in taxes, tactical changes need to be handled with caution.
- In order to make intelligent judgments about tactical allocation, advisors need to understand what is going on in the world and how that affects capital markets and areas of risk and reward. Advisors who lack insights into the capital markets will fail to evolve a family's portfolio appropriately.
- The challenge of finding and monitoring money managers who will outperform in the future (rather than just the past) is a huge one for any advisor, but the challenge is magnified for advisors working with the ultra-rich. Issues that need to be considered include the tax efficiency of the manager's investment activities, the liquidity of the investment, the willingness of the manager to incorporate a family's specific tax needs (by trading specific tax lots, for example), and similar matters.
- Assessing the performance of a portfolio on a periodic basis (and increasingly in real time) is both a science and an art. Regulators require that these reports be accurate and that they follow certain standards for computing returns. But preparing reports that families can understand and use is very much an art form.
- Ultra-wealthy families will often need additional help in areas that are not core to an advisor's skill set. Nonetheless, advisors must understand these issues well enough to help the family think them through, at which point specific experts can be engaged. These areas might include setting up a family governance framework; assisting a family in thinking through its philanthropic goals and the various ways those goals can be carried out; working out complicated family dynamics issues that will ultimately determine

whether the family stays together or splits up; various issues associated with rising generations, including education about stewardship; socially responsible investing, which can be especially important to younger generations; structuring a family office, including which activities to bring in-house and which to outsource; and a thorough understanding of trusts and estates issues, especially including the many tax-motivated vehicles available to wealthy families.

* * *

I have attempted to write this book at a level such that it can be used by financial advisors who are already experienced and knowledgeable, but who have not yet worked with the ultra-wealthy, and by members of wealthy families who are seriously involved in the management of their family's affairs.

Let's get started on this journey together.

2

How Families Get Rich (and Why It Matters to You)

This brief chapter is designed to emphasize one very important point: *how* families make their money is directly related to the kinds of challenges their advisors will face early in the relationship. Those specific challenges will be addressed in greater detail later in the book, but the issue itself deserves to be emphasized.

Newly Wealthy Families

In a reasonably fair society—most of the world's developed free market democracies, for example—the main way to become rich is to sell something that other people want to buy. It might be a product or service that makes people happy (Walt Disney), something that makes their lives easier and richer (Google, Apple), something that is a staple of their lives (Heinz), or something that offers them a better place to live or work (real estate). It might be something we did not even know we wanted until some family started selling it (hula hoops).

Whatever it was that the family was selling, it was likely sold through a corporation, and if that company was well-run and its product or service was continuously improved, over time the value of the company grew. The family's company might have become fabulously valuable very quickly, as was the case with Google and Apple. More likely, the company's value would have grown gradually over a long period of years—a period often measured in generations.

© The Author(s) 2020
G. Curtis, *Advising the Ultra-Wealthy*, https://doi.org/10.1007/978-3-030-57605-9_2

Eventually, the company will be sold and this event will prove to be a defining moment in the life of the family. Quite suddenly, the family no longer owns an operating business. Instead, they own a large sum of liquid capital, which is a very different thing.

In addition, it was probably the case that many or even most family members would have worked for the family company. Now, after spending what might have been generations building the company, family members have no jobs.

Typically, it will be at this point that the family will seek a financial advisor, and hence, the advisor will enter the picture at a crucial and somewhat chaotic time. This is quite different from the experience an advisor has with smaller families, where the precipitating event in seeking an advisor will likely have been far less disruptive.

Thus it is that the issue of "how families *get* rich" is inextricably entwined with the challenge of "how families *stay* rich." The family is, in effect, being introduced to the world of liquid wealth at the same time that it is faced with the challenge of managing that wealth. And in most cases, the family will have had little, if any, experience with liquid portfolios.

Throughout this book, I devote many chapters to the issues ultra-wealthy families face, whether they are newly wealthy or are members of generations quite remote from the family members who built and sold the company. But for the *newly* wealthy (in liquid capital terms), these are some of the most urgent challenges:

- Giving serious thought to how the family's human capital will be preserved and, if possible, increased down through the generations. Human capital includes intellectual capital, emotional capital, spiritual capital, and so on.
- Designing a governance structure that will allow the family to make decisions that are both sound and widely accepted by other family members.
- Establishing a family office.
- Coming to grips with the risks and returns associated with owning and managing a large sum of liquid capital.
- Establishing a sensible spending plan for the family as a whole and for each family unit.
- Approving a long-term investment strategy that is appropriate for the family's risk tolerance, spending needs, and investment time horizon.
- Engaging money managers, including separate account managers, index funds or ETFs, hedge funds, real estate, and private equity partnerships.
- Adopting written policies that will guide the family and its portfolio through the years, including individual policy statements for investments

and spending, and perhaps a family vision statement or similar document focused on the family's ultimate legacy.
- Forming an investment committee.

In other words, no sensible family simply takes its new-found liquidity and dumps it into the market, with or without advice. The infrastructure described above is far more important in the long run than getting quickly invested or even how well the money is invested.

To take an extreme example, imagine a family that puts the infrastructure in place but thereafter underperforms its investment benchmarks for years. That family will, nonetheless, still be wealthy many generations from now.

Contrast that with a family that neglects the infrastructure but, by chance, happens to invest its money soundly. That family will be poor again in two more generations because good investment returns can't compensate for poor governance, lack of long-term thinking, and neglect of the family's human capital. That neglect will destroy the family very quickly.

Inherited Wealth

It's relatively unusual for a wealth advisor to gain a new client whose family has been wealthy in liquid terms for several generations, but it does happen. It might be that an already wealthy family has had a new, very substantial, liquidity event. It might be that the family is breaking up and individual family branches are seeking their own advisors. It might be that the family has become so unhappy with their former advisor that they wish to make a change. (This happens regularly when an advisory firm is sold or collapses or when a radical market event, like the Global Financial Crisis, exposes the weaknesses in what formerly seemed like a successful investment strategy.)

However it happens, a new client who has inherited its wealth will present similar, but also rather different, challenges for advisors. For example, odd as it seems, even a family with very old wealth may not have in place the infrastructure described above. Indeed, if the family is breaking up, that is one likely reason why it is happening.

It is also possible that whatever policies and practices *are* in place no longer serve the family's interests and need to be changed. Even the family office itself may need to be re-evaluated. Over the decades, family offices evolve and change, and capabilities that were formerly important may no longer be relevant or, if relevant, may be better outsourced. Other capabilities that were never part of the family office's mandate may now be urgently important.

Typically, the most immediate challenge for a new advisor to a long-wealthy family is to deal with the existing investment strategies and money managers. Consider a family that has long employed an old-line trust company to manage their wealth. In such a case, the investment strategy is likely to be too cautious and rather out-of-date. On top of that, the trust company will likely have been using its own (probably mediocre) in-house investment products.

New advisors to such families will have to design new strategies, introduce the families to new risks, and select superior money managers on as tax-efficient a basis as possible. None of this will be easy.

It is also possible—sad to say—that the current generation of family members may have been thoroughly spoiled by their experience of being wealthy since birth and having parents and grandparents who were wealthy from birth. In many such families, no one has held an actual job for generations, and the very idea of working for a living may be an utterly foreign idea. If the scale of the wealth, having been divided and subdivided over the years, is now no longer able to support the current generation and that generation will have to work for a living, matters could quickly get complicated.

Fortunately, my experience has been that even people who have been spoiled by wealth are rarely irredeemable. But even if they are up to the new challenges, these individuals will usually require a substantial period of time to adjust to the new reality. Just as newly wealthy people (tech millionaires, lottery winners) often adapt to their wealth only very gradually, so newly *less-*wealthy people will also require time to adjust.

Conclusion

Every company in America, no matter how large it may be today, was once a small, fragile enterprise founded by a hopeful family. Most new businesses fail—roughly four out of five of them, in fact. Only a tiny minority succeed and grow beyond the mom-and-pop phase.

The stories behind each of these successful companies is fascinating, and one of the great pleasures of working with the ultra-wealthy is that their advisors have the opportunity to learn the remarkable stories and get to know some of the remarkable people behind them.

But however successful a family has become, and however large their liquid capital may now be, the transition from owning a company to owning liquid capital is hugely challenging. The early months and years following the sale event will be crucial to the family's ability to be as successful as investors as they were as company owners.

Advisors to such families play a crucial role in helping them navigate the many challenges of the new world they are inhabiting. If those challenges can be successfully surmounted, the family and the advisor are likely to have a long and fruitful relationship. Indeed, many of these relationships will be measured in generations.

3

Differences Between Wealthy Families and Institutions

Because of the scale of capital they control, ultra-wealthy families can appear to be superficially similar to institutions. Indeed, many families boast institution-like trappings: rigorous governance and decision-making systems, for example. Larger families may also employ a chief investment officer and even a few investment analysts. Family boards and investment committees are entities descended from similar entities at institutions. Finally, many families pursue investment strategies that are commonly associated with very large, sophisticated institutional investors, that is, modest exposures to fixed income assets and high exposure to alternative assets like hedge, private equity, and real estate.

But advisors who aspire to work with wealthy families need to keep firmly in mind that the superficial similarities between families and institutions are just that—superficial. In fact, families that control hundreds of millions of dollars are more similar to the advisors' own families than they are to institutions. Families, after all, are families, and the dynamics of kinship overwhelm the scale of the wealth.

Let's survey some of the principal differences between families and institutions.

Taxes

Unlike institutional investors, wealthy investors pay taxes—often very high taxes and via quite complex tax regimes: ordinary income taxes, capital gains taxes, gift and estate taxes. They pay taxes at the international level (especially

© The Author(s) 2020
G. Curtis, *Advising the Ultra-Wealthy*, https://doi.org/10.1007/978-3-030-57605-9_3

investment-related taxes), and at the federal, state, and local levels. Families based outside the US can also face complex tax issues, depending on where they live, where their assets are based, and how those assets are held.

Most institutions pay no taxes at all. Private foundations (and certain charitable trusts) pay a small excise tax, but even that tax can be reduced through careful management of the giving program. It is true that the US Congress has considered imposing a similar excise tax on certain large, endowed universities, but the proposed tax is quite small, at 1.4%, and it affects only a small number of large endowed universities.

While it would be unwise for families to be tax-driven in their investment activities, it would be even more unwise for family investors to ignore the consequences of taxes. Jack Bogle, the founder of Vanguard Investments, has estimated that taxes can easily eat up 2% of a family's investment return—that is some serious tax drag!

As a result, most wealthy families will spend a great deal of time and effort trying to take advantage of every lawful method for reducing taxes, including trusts, charitable gifting, grantor retained annuity trusts (GRATs), discounted intra-family gifting, strategies designed to move assets out of the estates of older family members, and so on. One result of these efforts is that most wealthy families will end up with massively complex portfolios.

Complexity

Speaking of complexity, institutional investors are almost always vastly simpler entities to manage from an investment perspective. Most of the time, an institutional endowment will consist of only one pot of money that can be managed as a whole. As just noted above, however, wealthy families almost always have many separate portfolios and investment vehicles with different objectives, time horizons, tax characteristics, and so on. Today, it's also not uncommon for wealthy families to have family members who are domesticated in or at least resident in different countries. This adds complexity, but also offers the possibility for tax arbitrage.

A wealthy family in the US might easily have investable assets held in individual names, in joint names, in the names of members of different generations or collateral relatives, in family investment partnerships and family limited partnerships, in charitable foundations, family trusts, IRAs, closely held corporations limited liability companies (LLCs), offshore vehicles, intentionally defective grantor trusts, dynasty trusts, and in a very large variety of tax-motivated entities such as chartable lead trusts, charitable remainder trusts, and the alphabet soup of tax and charitable vehicles such as GRATs, GRUTs, CRATs, CLATs, CLUTs, charitable remainder unit trusts (CRUTs), NIMCRUTs, and so on.

Wealthy families domesticated outside the US can have complicated estates as well. Assets might be held in the local equivalent of trusts (*fiducie*, in France, for example), in offshore accounts, in *anstalts* (a kind of hybrid between a corporation and a trust), and similar vehicles.

Nature of the Advisory Community

Typically, different kinds of advisors represent wealthy families than are found advising institutional portfolios, although of course there is overlap. Almost all wealth advisors will also have at least a few institutional clients, and almost all institutional advisors will have a few wealthy family clients. For one thing, most ultra-wealthy families will have private foundations, and those vehicles are low-tax institutional investors.

Historically, wealthy families had their assets managed by banks and trust companies. It is only in the last quarter century or so that independent wealth advisory firms have formed to offer wealthy families the same kind of sophisticated, objective advice that institutions have enjoyed for almost half a century.

Outside the US the advisory community continues to center on the global banks, but that is slowly changing as foreign investors better understand the conflicts of interest inherent in that business model.

To be credible as advisors to the ultra-wealthy, financial advisors should focus heavily on families and not pretend that they can be all things to all investors. In particular, institutional investment consulting firms have an unfortunate habit of treating their family clients like institutions.

If a predominantly institutional advisory firm wishes to be credible as a family advisor, it will need to establish a family-only division populated with advisors who have extensive experience advising families. The same is true of family advisory firms who wish to develop credibility with institutional advisors. But because families are so much more complicated than institutions, it's easier for a family advisor to work with institutional investors than the other way around.

Money Managers

Wealthy investors will tend to work with money managers that differ both from those used by both smaller investors (typically mutual funds, index funds and exchange-traded funds) and by institutional investors. This follows partly as a matter of law and regulation: many managers can only be accessed by sophisticated investors who possess incomes and net worths that are much higher than is typically found among middle-income investors. (These are the "accredited investor" and "qualified purchaser" rules.)

Beyond that, many of the best money managers enforce minimum account sizes that make them unavailable to smaller investors. This is especially true of private equity, venture capital, and hedge funds, but it can also be true of some emerging markets and municipal bond managers, as well as other niche funds.

While wealthy investors can usually gain access to the same exclusive money managers available to institutional investors, wealthy investors will want to work only with a subset of those managers, namely those who are willing and able to take tax consequences into account in their management styles. For example, the managers should be willing to select the lowest-tax securities to sell (i.e., use tax-lot accounting), should be aware of holding periods (not selling a stock just before it would become a long-term gain, for example), and should be willing to engage in tax loss selling even if it might slightly reduce the managers' return.

Most US-based wealthy families will use money managers based all over the world, although their assets will likely be held in custody in the US. Foreign families may use custodians in both their local jurisdiction and also offshore jurisdictions. Institutional custody is usually much simpler and cheaper.

Absolute Return Investors

Wealthy investors have a very different relationship with their capital than do institutional investors, and this may be the single most important distinction between the two.

Wealthy families earned their capital through many years—often many generations—of hard work, work that was performed by ancestors and nearer relatives that share DNA with the current generation of the family. Thus, even if the company that produces the wealth has been sold, the capital remains deeply embedded in the emotional makeup of the family.

Institutional capital isn't owned by any human person; it is "owned" by a fictional entity—a college or university, a foundation, an endowed nonprofit organization, or a pension plan. The human persons who manage the institution's capital come and go over time as they rotate onto and off of boards and investment committees. Most of these people are volunteers, and while they usually take their responsibilities seriously, it simply isn't possible for them to care as much about an institution's capital as a family cares about its own capital.

This is one reason why institutions tend to be "relative return investors" while families tend to be "absolute return investors." Relative return investors care more about how well they are doing versus their peers—other universities, for example—than they do about how well they are doing on an absolute basis. To take an extreme example, if during the Financial Crisis a university endowment lost 35% of its value in 1 year, that might or might not be a huge problem. If peer universities were down 40%, the university is probably happy.

However, no family will be happy to be down 35% in 1 year, no matter what is happening with other families or other investors. Hence, families, being absolute return investors, will tend to adopt strategies that are more capital-preservation-oriented than the strategies employed by similarly sized institutional investors.

Another reason for the difference in how families and institutions relate to their capital has to do with the fact that much institutional capital is replaceable. If an institution loses a significant amount of its endowment in the markets, it can simply ask its advancement office to launch a capital campaign. (As these words were being written, Harvard University, one of the poorer-performing endowments in recent years, announced that it had raised *$9.6 billion* in its current capital campaign.)

Families, needless to say, have no such luxury. Large losses often represent permanent losses of capital for a wealthy family. And since that capital was the result of long years of effort by family members, the loss is felt very keenly.

Non-Investment Issues Really Matter

When the management of a wealthy family's investment portfolio produces very poor results, the culprit is unlikely to be poor investment advice. Instead, the culprit is more likely to be family disruption: disputes among family members, inattention, poor family governance and decision-making, decline in human capital, and so on.

An institutional investor can certainly have dysfunctional governance—indeed, many institutions are very poorly governed, both in terms of their investment decision-making and more broadly. But families simply have many more ways to go wrong.

Thus, while aspiring wealth advisors will need to master many of the same subject areas as institutional advisors—especially efficient market theory and behavioral finance—they will need to master many other, related disciplines as well. A wealth advisor is part investment advisor, part tax advisor, part organizational and decision-making expert, and part confidant.

Wealth Tends to Dominate Everything

Even if a wealthy family member is a successful professional person, his or her income is likely to represent a small fraction of the income and wealth produced by the family's investment portfolio. Members of wealthy families work because work is important, because work allows them to be productive citizens wholly apart from their financial wealth, and because work structures their lives and gives those lives meaning beyond wealth.

But the wealth is always there and looms over everything. Like smaller families, wealthy families often have IRA accounts, purchase homes, pay college expenses for their children, and so on. But these issues play far less crucial roles for wealthy families, since even substantial expenses can often be paid out of the annual income from the family's portfolio or out of distributions from trust accounts. Thus, it is the sound management of the family's investment capital that truly matters.

By contrast, for most endowed institutions, the management of the portfolio is a secondary matter relative to the time and effort devoted to the institution's core mission.

Conclusion

Although ultra-wealthy families and institutions can seem to be similar, there are vast differences. Some of these differences directly affect the kinds of strategies and managers appropriate for families, but the more profound differences have to do with the nature of families, their complexity, their rapid evolution as people are born, grow up, marry, have children, divorce, remarry, grow old and die.

Prospective advisors to wealthy families will need to approach those families very differently than they would approach a similarly sized institutional investor.

4

Building an Ultra-Wealthy Family Client Base

Financial advisors who aspire to work with the ultra-wealthy often despair of making it happen. After all, they seem to be caught in an impossible catch-22: on the one hand, no wealthy family will hire them if they have no experience advising the wealthy; on the other hand, if no wealthy family will hire them, they will never get the necessary experience.

In fact, there are many possible paths to building a successful wealth advisory business and I will describe a few of them in this chapter.

Working Your Way Up

A great many people who have built successful wealth management businesses started at the bottom and worked their way up. You might begin as a very young advisor in a bank that offers financial advisory services to a wide range of families. You will start by working (under supervision, of course) with smaller families, but if you are diligent, you will work your way up. Eventually, you will be working with the largest and most sophisticated families at the bank.

At that point it will almost always be possible for you to go off on your own—forming your own wealth advisory firm anchored by a few clients who follow you from the bank. Alternatively, you may be recruited by an existing wealth advisory firm and may or may not take clients with you.

Notice that most banks (and similar firms) will insist that you sign a non-compete agreement, preventing you from taking the bank's clients or employees for some period of time and even preventing you from engaging in a

© The Author(s) 2020
G. Curtis, *Advising the Ultra-Wealthy*, https://doi.org/10.1007/978-3-030-57605-9_4

wealth management business at all for a period of years in a specific geographical area.

Some of these contracts are quite stringent and may be fully enforceable in
the state where the bank's office is located. But most noncompete agreements
are carefully and narrowly drafted to withstand legal scrutiny. Many state
courts frown on noncompete agreements that are too broadly drawn, and in
some states it's very difficult to draft a noncompete that will withstand
scrutiny.

In any event, almost all noncompete agreements can be worked around. As
a simple example, the agreement may prevent you from contacting the bank's
clients in an attempt to recruit them. But the bank can't prevent clients with
whom you have developed a close relationship from contacting *you* and engaging you as their new advisor.

Recruiting Wealthy Family Clients to Your Existing Advisory Firm

Catch-22s notwithstanding, it is often surprisingly easy for a traditional financial planning firm to recruit a wealthy family as a client. This is because, for a
great many families, issues like experience and even skill levels are less important than another factor: *trust.*

Thus, advisors who already operate a financial planning firm but who aspire
to work with the ultra-wealthy simply need to organize their lives around
opportunities to meet and gain the trust of such families. Here are a few
examples of activities that are likely to prove fruitful:

- Join country clubs, business clubs, and other organizations where members
  of wealthy families tend to collect. Become social acquaintances of these
  people and, over the years, offer them free and good advice about financial
  and investment issues. When/if they are looking for a new advisor, they will
  put your firm in the mix.
- Join boards of trustees of not-for-profit organizations: colleges and universities, symphonies and operas, arts and other cultural groups, organizations
  devoted to helping the disadvantaged. Members of wealthy families gravi-
  tate to the boards of such organizations, and if you are a strong board
  member, you will find many opportunities to impress those people.
- Join organizations that include many business owners—YPO, for example.
  While these people may not be wealthy yet, they are likely to become

wealthy as their businesses grow and are sold. You will find yourself prominently on the list of potential advisors.

• Accept clients whose investment assets are very small, but who own businesses or are involved in activities like real estate development, even if you have to waive your minimum account size. When/if these businesses become successful, you will already have the client.

Demonstrate Your Intellectual Capital

It's essentially impossible to market your services to wealthy families in any normal way. Advertising doesn't work, cold calling is a joke. It's often difficult even to know who is ultra-wealthy and who is just a successful upper middle-class person.

One way to deal with this problem is to let wealthy families find their way to you, not the other way around. Members of those families love to read well-written and informative (and, preferably, short) articles about investment and other financial issues, as well as about family issues.

You could develop a monthly newsletter, write a blog, write articles for local newspapers or magazines, even write a book(!) These activities will get your name out there and members of wealthy families will notice.

Cultivate COIs

"COIs" are centers of influence, that is, people who work with wealthy families in one way or another and who have influence on their buying decisions. The most obvious COIs are attorneys (especially trust and estate lawyers, but also lawyers who advise family businesses or sales of family businesses). But don't overlook tax accountants, investment bankers, even money managers.

Cultivating COIs is certainly a challenge. Such people are busy professionals and you will hardly be the only financial advisor vying for their time and attention. The secrets to success in this endeavor are twofold: first, *make yourself useful* to such people. Don't take up their time telling them how wonderful you are—instead, offer them information they can use in their own professional activities, information that will help them look good to their clients.

Second, focus on *reciprocity*. If you can refer business to the COIs, they will be far more likely to refer business to you.

A Note About Credentialing

In working with smaller families, credentials can be important. Financial columnists and commentators generally recommend that investors work only with financial advisors who have been credentialed. Hence the profusion of designations such as the CFP® (Certified Financial Planner), ChFC (Chartered Financial Consultant), AIF® (Accredited Investment Fiduciary), CLU (Chartered Life Underwriter), CAIA (Chartered Alternative Investment Analyst), CMFC (Chartered Mutual Fund Counselor), CIMA® (Certified Investment Management Analyst), and so on.

But it's a different world when marketing yourself to the ultra-wealthy. Less-sophisticated investors need something to help them assess whether advisors know what they're talking about, but ultra-wealthy families couldn't care less. They have recourse to a vast bevy of people who can vet wealth advisors: lawyers, accountants, bankers, family office personnel, and, especially, other wealthy families. On top of that, many wealthy families will use elaborate RFPs (requests for proposals) designed to ferret out everything about you and your firm.

It is certainly true that most advisors to ultra-wealthy families have some sort of credential, but they tend to be these: JD, MBA, CPA, CFA (Chartered Financial Analyst). In fact, you may well find that when you are pitching a wealthy family, the usual certifications (CFP®, for example) would be better left off your signature block, since they tend to suggest "retail" to wealthy families and their other advisors.

The real reason to get yourself credentialed is to learn the skills the designation represents. But those designations will be of very little, if any, help in *marketing* to the ultra-wealthy.

Make Sure You Have What You Need

It won't do you any good to follow the above advice, snag a wealthy client, and then make a mess of it. Word about that unfortunate event will travel through the wealth community very quickly.

If you want to build a competitive national or international wealth advisory firm, you will have to build it out very significantly, and that will cost a lot of money and take a lot of time. (Although, of course, you can do this gradually, using existing cash flow.)

But to handle your first few wealthy families successfully requires surprisingly modest improvements in your skill set, operations, and personnel, especially if your first few clients are newly wealthy and don't have a lot of built-in expectations.

For example, many of the investments wealthy families use are the same as those used by other investors. Cheap, passive mutual funds and ETFs purchased to gain exposure to efficient asset classes is one example.

Or consider municipal bonds. Smaller investors will typically use mutual funds to gain municipal bond exposure, but the firms that manage those funds often have separately managed accounts that follow the same investment style. A new wealthy family client will likely want a separate account, but since you already know the bond firm it's a simple matter to invest in the separate account product, rather than the mutual fund version.

Real estate can be a bit trickier. A core real estate exposure for a wealthy family will often look very similar to a core real estate exposure for a smaller client. But core real estate often becomes overvalued, and niche real estate tends to be a different animal, often offered not as a traditional managed fund but in hedge fund format or even in a drawdown vehicle similar to a private equity fund.

Large wealth management firms will know where to find these niche products, but even if you have only one wealthy family client you will at least be able to give them core real estate exposure, and the manager of the core product may also offer niche products. These might include specialized real estate sectors that haven't become overpriced, such as storage, university housing, or distressed real estate.

A wealthy family should have an exposure to hedge funds, and most smaller financial advisory firms won't have the skill set to perform appropriate diligence on those funds. And they require a *lot* of diligence, both upfront (before the client invests) and ongoing (while the client is invested).

One way around this is to use hedge funds of funds at first, while you are building up your own hedge fund diligence capability. Funds of funds aren't ideal—the double layer of fees eats up return—but the best of them are better than nothing.

Venture capital and private equity are also asset classes the wealthy need to have, and here, in addition to the skill-set issue, there are other challenges as well. For example, there is the challenge of gaining access to the best funds, and there is the challenge of building in diversification for your client: vintage year diversification, sector diversification, geographical diversification, and so on. As with hedge funds, funds of funds will likely be your go-to solution at first.

Performance reporting can also be a challenge. A wealthy family may want to see their performance from several different angles. There is the performance of the managers, the performance of the sectors, appropriate benchmarks for everything, finding ways of showing performance on a risk-adjusted basis, and so on. You will likely find it necessary to invest more in this side of your business, at least if you intend to continue to build an ultra-wealthy client base.

Wealthy families also need more than investment advice. They will want to talk with you about how best to govern their family, how to make good decisions, how to involve younger family members, and many other issues. If you can educate yourself about these issues and be helpful to your wealthy clients, those clients will become very sticky and will also recommend you to other wealthy families.

Along the same lines, it will be useful for you to educate yourself about specialized firms that can help wealthy families with issues like intergenerational rivalries, family business disputes, and philanthropic advice.

Finally, a word about cybersecurity. All financial advisory firms need to worry about cybersecurity and to take steps to protect themselves and their clients—the Securities and Exchange Commission and the states are all over this issue. But the problem becomes much more magnified when you are advising wealthy clients. A cybersecurity problem can result in huge losses, and wealthy families are much more desirable targets for scammers than ordinary households. You might even want to look into buying a cybersecurity insurance policy.

Conclusion

Somewhat surprisingly, it isn't all that difficult to get and keep a wealthy family or two. There are workarounds—some of them are described above—that can help, and many newly wealthy families don't really know what to expect in any event.

Of course, if you want to build a nationally competitive wealth advisory business you will need to do more than just get by. You will need to implement best practices across the board. Fortunately, that doesn't need to happen overnight. Many successful wealth advisory firms were built over the course of several decades.

5

A Wealthy Family's Many Advisors

If you want to build a successful business advising ultra-wealthy families, you will need to become familiar with the vast and complex world of *non*financial advisors to such families.

Just as the portfolios of wealthy families are famously complex, so too are most of the other affairs of such families. Financial advisors need to know who these other advisors are, how to find them, when to bring them into the mix, and how to work constructively with them.

It may seem to you that the family's various advisors are focused on discrete (and discreet!) issues and that there should be little overlap with what you are doing. But remember that families rarely see things that way. They will raise tax issues with the investment advisor, philanthropic issues with the lawyer, and family dynamics issues with the banker.

In this chapter, I describe some of the non-investment advisors you are likely to encounter in your work with ultra-wealthy families.

Attorneys

Wealthy families won't just have one attorney, they will usually have many. Someone will oversee trust and estate planning for the family, someone else will handle real estate issues, and still others will be retained to advise on matters related to the family business, on litigation, international law, tax, and so on. Ideally, one trusted attorney will quarterback all these lawyers and make sure the family is being well-advised overall. That was certainly the way it used to be.

© The Author(s) 2020
G. Curtis, *Advising the Ultra-Wealthy*, https://doi.org/10.1007/978-3-030-57605-9_5

These days, however, families will often seek out the best legal talent available, regardless of which firm the attorneys are associated with or even which city they reside in. In those cases, it might fall to you—the financial advisor—to coordinate the activities of the various attorneys and to make sure the family isn't being overbilled or otherwise taken advantage of.

Moreover, if a family is newly wealthy—having just sold their business, for example—you may be the one they turn to recommend the best legal talent for each issue the family faces. Fortunately, this is usually easier than it sounds. If you speak to enough people the same legal names will come up over and over again, and as you gain experience working with wealthy families you will see for yourself which attorneys provide good advice at a reasonable price and which don't.

In rare cases (especially in Boston for some reason), law firms can be competitors of yours, as a few firms have branched out into the wealth advisory business. For the most part, however, you should be able to work with a family's legal advisors fairly smoothly.

For example, the family's trust and estates lawyer will work closely with you on the estate plan, making sure you know what the tax characteristics are of the various estate planning vehicles. For tax reasons, some trusts are very sensitive to receiving income earned in certain states. Some trusts are structured as "grantor trusts," meaning that the grantor pays the income tax, not the trust or the beneficiary, and so on.

Tax Accountants

Every wealthy family will employ a tax accountant to handle its complex tax issues, ensuring both that it is in compliance with the maddeningly complex tax code and also that it is paying no more tax than necessary. Occasionally the tax advisor will be a lawyer, but few lawyers will actually be filling out tax returns. More typically, tax lawyers will be brought in to advise on especially complicated tax problems.

As the family's financial advisor, you will interact with the tax accountants on a regular basis. They will need information from you about the tax consequences of the investments you have recommended to the family, and you will need information from them about the tax status of the various family members.

Unlike attorneys, accountants very often have wealth management businesses of their own. If not, they may work closely with a wealth advisory firm and consistently refer business to that firm. As with other types of "consulting" work done by accounting firms, many people believe that it is a conflict of interest for tax accountants to act as financial advisors to the same family. However, the accounting watchdogs haven't yet prohibited this kind of work.

Note that sophisticated tax accountants will come up with an almost unlimited number and variety of tax-motivated ideas: dynasty trusts, chartable lead trusts, charitable remainder trusts, GRATs, GRUTs, CRATs, CLATs, CLUTs, CRUTs, NIMCRUTs, and so on. Many of these vehicles are quite useful, and it will fall to you to structure the investments correctly for each vehicle. But this practice can also get out of hand. At some point, complexity overcomes tax savings, and you will need to be alert to where that point lies.

Bankers

Families will typically have one lead bank they tend to work with, although if the family owns a business, there may be completely different people or institutions banking the company.

For families, banking services will include providing bank accounts, lending facilities, jumbo mortgages, cash management, brokerage, and so on. For the company similar services will be offered, along with management of the company's cash, currency hedging, and similar services.

Needless to say, many banks also offer wealth advisory services, although most smaller or regional banks are not typically competitive in the ultra-wealthy space. But the big money center banks—JP Morgan Chase, BNY Mellon, Bank of America, Citi—certainly offer competitive wealth management advice, as do some of the super regionals like PNC, US Bancorp, and Wells Fargo.

Some banks, especially the larger trust and custodian banks, will respect your relationship with the client, but the other banks are quite different and may try to steal the client as soon as you take your eyes off the ball. Be forewarned.

Investment Bankers

If the family owns a company it may employ investment bankers to advise on mergers, acquisitions, restructurings, and similar activities. The list of so-called I-banks is long and includes global players like Goldman Sachs and

Morgan Stanley, along with powerful regional or middle market players like Jeffries, Baird, and others.

This is a highly specialized business not closely related to the wealth advisory work you do. However, almost all these banks also offer wealth advisory services. Very often, when a family sells its business, they will almost automatically hire the I-bank's wealth advisory team. Even if they don't, that team is likely to be in the mix competing against you.

Custodians

As you know, a custodian holds a family's assets. In other words, money managers will manage the assets entrusted to them (making buy-sell decisions), but the assets will remain in the hands of the custodian. (It is a *very* bad practice to allow a manager to self-custody assets.)

Asset custody is a lousy business. It is low margin and requires huge capital investment both upfront and on an ongoing basis to remain competitive. The only reason banks offer the service is as a loss-leader—if a family is custodied at a bank, the family is highly likely to use at least some of the bank's investment products.

For families the business is dominated by a very few institutions: BNY Mellon, Northern Trust, and, for certain families, Fidelity and Schwab. Many other banks offer custody, but they are mostly not very good at it, having decided not to invest in the required technology or to keep it up to date and competitive.

Since families are taxable, and since they often use family limited partnerships or LLCs as common investment vehicles, a good custodian is essential. Not only must the custodian keep accurate records, but the taxation of investment partnerships is complicated. If the custodian can't or won't provide partnership tax accounting, the family will have to engage an accounting firm to handle the accounting, and that can get very expensive.

Although custody is cheap, a good custodian is worth its weight in gold. Therefore, it will often make sense for you to use at least some of the custodian's investment products to keep them happy. Custody banks often have at least a few products that are competitive—fixed income and index funds, for example.

Other Family Advisors

In addition to the above, families will often find it useful to engage advisors to assist them with other issues: family dynamics, succession, governance, philanthropy, even bill paying. Since these types of advisors aren't used as regularly as the more traditional advisors described above, families will often be at a loss for where to find them. You can perform a very useful service by keeping a short list of the best firms or individuals operating in each of the areas mentioned.

Conclusion

The affairs of ultra-wealthy families are enormously complex, and those families require a broad spectrum of advisory services. Those advisors need to work smoothly together, to cooperate and to share necessary information. If, as the family's wealth advisor, you can position yourself as the quarterback overseeing this bevy of advisors, you can cement your relationship with the family while assuring that they receive the best service, regardless of the discipline.

6

Policy Statements for Wealthy Families

An ultra-wealthy family's financial affairs are enormously complex, and without written policy statements both the family and its advisors are likely to be at sea. There are four types of policy statements that are crucial for most families.

The Investment Policy Statement You are clearly experienced at preparing investment policy statements (IPSs) for your clients, but you should probably draft a more complex form of IPS for your ultra-wealthy clients. The ultra-wealthy family IPS won't necessarily cover different material, but it will cover that material in more depth. In addition, the IPS should probably be more discursive and descriptive than a typical IPS for a retail or affluent client.

There are many reasons for these differences. In the first place, a wealthy family's portfolio will almost certainly be far more complex than other family portfolios. In addition, a wealthy family will be far more likely to use an investment committee, which will refer to the IPS regularly for guidance. Finally, wealthy families tend to think about their portfolios *dynastically*— that is, in a multigenerational way. Therefore, the IPS should be descriptive enough that a younger generation of family members can sit down, read it, and understand what is being talked about. A sample IPS is attached to this chapter as Exhibit A.

The Investment Committee Operating Manual In addition to the investment policy statement, if your client uses an investment committee, you should also prepare an investment committee operating manual (ICOM). The IPS tells the family where the portfolio should go, but the ICOM tells the

© The Author(s) 2020
G. Curtis, *Advising the Ultra-Wealthy*, https://doi.org/10.1007/978-3-030-57605-9_6

investment committee how to get there. It is essentially a seasonal agenda for the committee, designed to ensure that it stays on track, discharges its main duties, and doesn't get bogged down or sidetracked. A sample ICOM is attached to this chapter as Exhibit B.

The Spending Policy Statement Many families will also want to adopt a spending policy. The purpose of a spending policy is two-fold: it explains why controlling spending is so crucial, and it establishes a maximum withdrawal rate from the portfolio. Over-spending is one of the principal ways wealthy families cease to be wealthy. A sample spending policy is attached to this chapter as Exhibit C.

Manager Guidelines Finally, ultra-wealthy families will invest primarily through separate accounts opened with individual managers. Each of those accounts will need to have manager guidelines prepared. These guidelines tell both the manager and the family (or investment committee) how to manage the account and they also allow you to monitor compliance with the family's instructions. Every manager guideline will be different, of course, but a sample guideline is attached to this chapter as Exhibit D.

Exhibit A

Investment Policy Statement
Smith Family
Adopted _____ 20__

Purpose

The purpose of this investment policy statement (IPS) is to describe the investment objectives, risk tolerance, and spending policies of the Smith family and the investment policies, strategies, vehicles, and financial management procedures in sufficient detail to guide the family, their trustees, and their advisors in the management of the family's investments.

Background: The Smith Family

The Smith family, currently consisting of more than 50 individual family members and several hundred trusts, traces its roots back to the border area between France and Germany, specifically Alsace and Lorraine. A complete list of current living family members and family trusts, along with the tax treatment of each, is maintained by the Smith family office, SteelCon LLC, and is available at all times to the Investment Committee.

Alsace and Lorraine were contested for centuries by France and Germany, resulting in such chaos that the family's ancestor, Alphonse Smith, emigrated to America, arriving with less than $5 to his name.

Alphonse launched a small metalworking shop in Batavia, Illinois, that gradually, over three generations, grew into a large structural steel company. That company was sold in 2012, resulting in proceeds to the family, net after tax, of more than $500 million.

Today the senior generation of the Smith family—Charles W. Smith and his wife, Annie, and Franklin A. Smith and his wife, Odelle, all in their 70s—are the primary overseers of the family's wealth. Charles, Annie, and Franklin sit on the family's Investment Committee (described below) along with two members of the next generation (referred to in the family as G5), Sandy Ellington and Roger Smith. It is expected that over the next 5 years or so, all the family members of the Investment Committee will be G5s.

Charles and Franklin are currently co-CEOs of SteelCon, although it is anticipated that Sandy Ellington will replace Charles within the next few years and that Roger Smith will replace Franklin within 5–7 years.

Statement of Objectives and Constraints

Based on the Smith Family Values Statement, it is important for the managers of the family's capital to understand that the family values its intellectual, moral, and personal capital far more than its financial capital. The family well understands that "families grow faster than capital" and that, therefore, future family members will have far less wealth, per capita, than current family members. The family does not consider this to be an issue. Indeed, whenever the family's nonfinancial capital and financial capital come into conflict, it will be the former that prevails.

Given the foregoing, the objective for the family's capital is to grow at approximately the rate of inflation as measured by the Consumer Price Index, while providing sufficient annual cash flow (or other form of appropriate liquidity) to support the family's spending, including gifts and taxes. That spending, in the aggregate, will not be allowed to exceed 3% of the value of the family's capital. In general, the family expects that its exposure to risk assets will rarely exceed 60% of total assets and that 50% will be the primary target.

Specific objectives and portfolio constraints:

1. The family can tolerate volatility but wishes to avoid permanent loss of capital. Diversification among asset classes, securities, strategies and managers (especially among hedge and private equity managers) is fundamental to the family's risk control.
2. The family seeks relative capital preservation during negative market environments and therefore anticipates participating less fully during positive market environments in an effort to achieve acceptable risk-adjusted returns over full market cycles.
3. The family recognizes that their objectives require risk of temporary capital loss. An acceptable parameter is no more than a 10% risk of a 25% or greater peak-to-trough decline in inflation-adjusted value over rolling 3-year periods. The family recognizes that it is possible that their portfolios modeled within this risk parameter will nevertheless at some time suffer a greater than 25% drawdown. Absent compelling reasons to the contrary the appropriate response will be to rebalance to policy allocations because of the likelihood of recovery.
4. The family seeks to maintain sufficient high-grade fixed income and cash to cover spending needs for at least 5 years during times of market distress in order to give markets time to recover. In addition, this liquidity is expected to be useful during periods of market distress when significant market inefficiencies are pronounced and make it possible to purchase high-quality investments at temporarily depressed prices. For those portfolios with significant commitments to private equity and other drawdown style investments, adequate liquidity will also be needed to ensure that outstanding capital commitments can be funded when capital is called during crisis periods.

Portfolio Performance

The family's portfolio results will be compared to three primary overall benchmarks:

1. Absolute Return Benchmark: As noted above, to grow at approximately the rate of inflation as measured by the Consumer Price Index, while providing sufficient annual cash flow (or other form of appropriate liquidity) to support the family's spending, including gifts and taxes.
2. Relative Return Benchmark: Pre-tax and net of investment expenses, to outperform, over rolling 3–5 year market cycles, a composite benchmark consisting of the weighted average of the asset class performance benchmarks established for the family's portfolio.
3. Reference Portfolio Benchmark: Pre-tax and net of investment expenses, to outperform a Reference Portfolio consisting of 50% Vanguard Total Stock Market Index (VTSMX) and 50% Vanguard California Intermediate-Term Tax-Exempt (VCAIX).

Division of Responsibilities

The Smith family portfolio is overseen by the SteelCon Investment Committee, whose members are appointed by the Board of Directors of SteelCon. The Investment Committee will always have a majority of family members, but may also include non-family members.

The SteelCon Board is ultimately accountable for the management of the family's capital but has determined that the portfolio is more likely to achieve its return objectives if oversight and management are delegated to an Investment Committee. Discretionary authority for all investment decisions resides with the Investment Committee, whose members are fiduciaries.

The Investment Committee may, and is expected to, engage an outside chief investment officer (OCIO) to work with the family's internal Chief Investment Officer. The duties of the OCIO, with immediate supervision by the CIO and overall supervision by the Investment Committee, are as follows:

1. Serving as a fiduciary in its advisory role with the family, placing the family's interests above its own, that is, to act in good faith and with the care, skill, prudence, and diligence, under the circumstances then prevailing, that a prudent person acting in a like capacity and position and familiar with these matters would use in the conduct of an enterprise such as the portfolio and with like aims.
2. Serving as the primary contact for all investment managers.
3. Performing investment due diligence and offering the Committee guidance in selecting, monitoring, and replacing the portfolio's investment managers.

4. Meeting with the Committee as requested to review the portfolio.
5. Providing periodic reports and updates to the Committee on the portfolio's performance and positioning, not less often than quarterly.
6. Providing ad hoc reports or analyses on various assets classes or investment opportunities as the Committee may request.
7. Providing necessary information to prepare reports and audits, in cooperation with SteelCon's accounting staff and external auditors, as and when needed.
8. Reporting to the Committee in writing any violations of the IPS or a material adverse change or finding related to the investment managers in the portfolio, or in the OCIO itself, as soon as it becomes aware of such change or violation.
9. Implementing the portfolio's investment strategy.

The Investment Committee's responsibilities are detailed in the Investment Committee Charter.

Investment Guidelines

The portfolio's investment strategy has been established in conjunction with a review of the Smith family's overall financial position, investment time horizon, risk tolerance, tax considerations, liquidity profile, and the diversification benefits of asset allocation.

Time Horizon
The investment guidelines of the portfolio are based upon a time horizon that is significantly greater than ten (10) years and more consistent with the family's generational planning. Therefore, interim portfolio fluctuations should be expected and viewed with appropriate perspective. Capital values fluctuate over shorter periods and the family recognizes that the possibility of capital loss exists.

Liquidity
SteelCon has determined that sufficient income and liquidity will be required from the portfolio given the illiquid nature of the family assets outside the portfolio. Further, SteelCon recognizes that individual family members may have the right to withdraw their capital from the portfolio at some point in the next 5 years. Therefore, the family's short-term cash needs must be

reflected in the cash levels and illiquidity constraints stipulated by the terms of this IPS. Specific anticipated cash needs and distributions are set forth in an exhibit to this IPS.

Given the liquidity and spending needs set forth above, under normal circumstances no more than [%] of the portfolio's net assets will be held in vehicles utilizing lockups of 1 year or longer. Lockup is defined as an expected period until all or substantially all of the value from an investment vehicle can be received in cash in the portfolio.

Portfolio Distributions

Under normal circumstances the Board may authorize a quarterly withdrawal of no more than [%] or an annual withdrawal of no more than 3% of the portfolio's net assets. The portfolio's liquidity should provide for these distributions without creating material misalignment or nonconformity with the disclosed terms of this IPS.

Under extraordinary circumstances, where distributions are required greater than the above, it should be expected that, for a period of time, the portfolio may not comply with all the terms of this IPS and/or distributions to owners may be satisfied with in-kind delivery of investment positions so as not to disadvantage the portfolio post-distribution, at the sole discretion of the Board.

Risk Tolerance

The Board has indicated a risk tolerance that aligns with a moderate risk profile. The Board understands that all investments involve the risk of loss, including the loss of principal, a reduction in earnings, and the loss of future earnings. Although this portfolio shall be managed in a manner consistent with the Board's risk tolerance, there can be no guarantee that these efforts will be successful. The Board should be prepared to bear the risk of loss.

Tax Considerations

In general, the portfolio will be managed by the Committee according to the Statement of Objectives above. However, it is important to highlight that to the extent that tax-advantaged strategies exist which the OCIO and Committee believe can be appropriate for the portfolio and consistent with the terms of this IPS, those strategies will be seriously considered. Items for consideration may include the nature of an asset's income or anticipated appreciation, or tax-loss harvesting opportunities; however, any tax consideration will be secondary to the primary objectives of this IPS.

Asset Allocation
One of the most important components of an investment strategy is the portfolio asset mix or the allocation among the various classes of securities and investment strategies available to the portfolio for investment purposes. The Committee will diversify investments among those asset classes and strategies, providing a balance of enhancing the total return of the portfolio while attempting to avoid undue risk concentration. It should be noted that a significant portion of an investment portfolio's variability of returns can be attributed to the asset allocation process. The Board has considered the risk, return, and correlation relationships between the major asset classes, as well as the portfolio's objectives, financial position, time horizon, risk tolerance, and tax consideration when constructing the following asset allocation policy.

The Committee, through the IPS, sets the long-term asset allocation targets and ranges. On a quarterly basis or as needed, the Committee shall recommend to the Board any changes to the asset allocation targets and ranges and the inclusion of any new asset classes. The Committee is permitted to allocate the assets within the range provided in Table A1 below.

Strategic Benchmark
Based on the Strategic Asset Allocation in Table A1, it is agreed that performance (net of all fees) should be measured against a blended benchmark. The Committee will set this benchmark consistent with the capital deployment (or phase-in) plan agreed to by the Board. The assigned benchmarks that will comprise the blended benchmark are as shown in Table A2.

Rebalancing
An asset class is considered to be within an acceptable range if the current allocation is within the lower and upper bands as discussed above. The actual allocation will be reviewed quarterly but may be changed at any time based on the judgment of the Committee.

Table A1 Strategic asset allocation

Asset class	Long-term Target allocation	Minimum	Maximum
Cash			
Fixed income			
Global equities			
Hedged strategies			
Private equity			
Real estate			
Commodities			

Table A2 Portfolio benchmarks

Asset class	Assigned benchmark
Cash	
Fixed income	
Global equities	
Hedged strategies	
Private equity	
Real estate	
Commodities	

There will be periodic deviations in actual asset weights from the long-term policy asset weights specified above. Causes for periodic deviations are market movements, cash flows, and varying portfolio performance. Significant movements from the asset class policy weights will alter the intended expected return and risk of the Fund. Accordingly, the Committee will collaborate with the OCIO to rebalance the portfolio when necessary to ensure adherence to the Investment IPS.

If an asset class allocation should move outside of its acceptable bands or might be reasonably expected to do so in the future, the OCIO shall notify the Committee of such event promptly. The OCIO will assess the trade-off between the cost of rebalancing and the active risk associated with the deviation from policy asset weights. With approval from the Committee, the OCIO may execute its recommendations or may delay a rebalancing program if the Committee believes the delay is in the best interest of the portfolio.

Asset Class Guidelines

The OCIO may recommend investment in individual securities, structured products, and/or one or more collective investment funds, such as commingled funds, mutual funds, or exchange-traded funds, or in one or more separately managed accounts representing the following asset classes:

Cash and Equivalents
Cash and cash equivalents provide stability and liquidity, particularly in times of high asset values. Investments such as money market mutual funds, money market accounts, and US Treasury Bills are examples of cash and cash-equivalent holdings. There is no guarantee that cash and cash equivalents will be fully FDIC insured.

Fixed Income

The strategic role of fixed income (bond) investments is to potentially diversify the portfolio's equity exposure. Bonds tend to exhibit low correlation to and lower volatility than stocks. Fixed income holdings may be invested across numerous markets, including, but not limited to, government, corporate, municipal, and agency bond markets, as well as global bond markets. Both investment-grade and non-investment grade (high-yield) securities may be used.

Global Equities

Global equities represent an ownership type of investment. The risks and expected returns tend to be higher than more secured investments such as cash and investment-grade bonds. The portfolio's equity exposure may be invested across US and non-US (emerging and developed) stock markets and across various sectors, styles, and company sizes depending on the economic environment at that time.

Hedged Strategies

Hedge funds are private investment pools employing sophisticated strategies that buy and sell equity and debt instruments, commodities, and derivatives. The non-traditional Hedged Strategies asset class encompasses a number of different investment strategies that are not necessarily available via long-only global equity strategies alone. The strategic role of a hedged strategy is to potentially diversify the portfolio's risk and/or enhance the portfolios returns. Hedged Strategies tend to carry greater investment risk, including, but not limited to, the fact that hedged investments may not be readily converted to cash.

Private Equity

Private equity is defined as investments in the equity and debt of privately held domestic and international companies. The strategic role of private equity in the portfolio is to potentially diversify the equity risk as well as potentially increase the expected return through allocation to managers who provide operational and financial expertise to companies in order to grow the enterprise value of the company or portion of the company acquired. Private equity tends to carry greater investment risk, including, but not limited to, the fact that private equity investments cannot be readily converted to cash.

Real Estate

Real estate may be included in a portfolio to potentially increase the return of a portfolio, to provide inflation protection, and to diversify the risk of a portfolio. Real estate exposure may be invested in both public and private investments as well as across multiple property types including but not limited to multi-family, office, hotel, and industrial. Private investments in real estate tend to carry greater investment risk, including but not limited to the fact that private real estate investments cannot be readily converted to cash.

Commodities

Commodities are generally assets related to food, energy, or metals. The strategic role of commodities is to offer further risk and return diversification, as well as potentially offer a hedge during times of inflation or uncertainty. Commodities may not be frequently recommended for the portfolio but may be selectively recommended in certain situations.

Restrictions

Restrictions on any actively managed separate accounts or other direct investments should incorporate a prohibition on any securities representing investment in:

(a) Any company that produces tobacco or tobacco-related products.
(b) Any security of GlobalCon, as the family already owns a very substantial amount of such securities.

Exhibit B

Investment Committee Operating Manual
Smith Family
Adopted _____ 20__

Purpose of the Manual

The purpose of this investment committee operating manual is to set forth policies and procedures to guide the deliberations of the Investment Committee of the Smith family. The Operating Manual is not designed to replace the family's investment policy statement (IPS), but to serve as a supplement to it. The IPS tells us where we want our portfolio to be, while the Operation Manual tells us what we need to do to get there and stay there.

Among other things, the Manual discusses the purposes of the Investment Committee and the relationship between the Committee and the family, the frequency of Committee meetings, and the general agenda for such meetings.

Long experience has shown that investment committees frequently make sub-optimal investment decisions. This outcome is an almost inevitable byproduct of the part-time nature of the committee's work, the frequent turn-over in personnel assigned to the committee, the tendency of all committees to act according to the "lowest common denominator," and the unstructured nature of most investment committee deliberations.

It is the hope of the Smith family that the existence of this Operating Manual and the Committee's determination to be guided by its provisions will help improve the operation of the Committee and redound to the benefit of the Smith family's investment capital and ultimate wealth.

Purpose of the Investment Committee

The purpose of the Investment Committee is to evaluate and make recommendations to the Smith family with regard to the investment policies and strategies to be followed by the family's investment portfolio, as follows:

1. The Committee will, via its own deliberations and through conversations with the family, determine an appropriate risk profile for the investment portfolio. It is understood that the degree of risk assumed will substantially determine the investment return available to the family.
2. The Committee will recommend investment policies to be followed in the management of the investment portfolio. These policies shall include (a) a long-term goal for the performance of the funds, (b) an asset allocation strategy designed to achieve the long-term goal, and (c) asset classes and types of investments which may be used in the investment of the portfolios.
3. The Committee will prepare and recommend to the family a written investment policy statement.
4. The Committee will prepare and recommend to the family a written spending policy. It is understood that spending by taxable families in excess of 4%—and preferably less—will have an important negative effect on the ability of the family to maintain and grow its wealth.
5. The Committee will prepare and recommend to the family written conflict of interest policies.
6. The Committee will recommend a management structure for the investment management and oversight of the family's investment portfolio. In

other words, the Committee will recommend whether the family should engage an investment consultant, should utilize the services of a master custodian, should employ independent managers, should manage the funds in-house, or follow some combination of both.

7. The Committee will monitor the level of expenses incurred in the management of the investment portfolio, including management fees, commissions and other transaction costs, and soft dollar arrangements, if any.
8. If necessary, the Committee will recommend a proxy voting procedure to the family.

In carrying out these important responsibilities, the Committee will be guided by the operating procedures set forth in this Manual.

Meetings of the Investment Committee

Unless otherwise determined by the Chair of the Committee, the Committee will meet three times per year, and at dates and times so established as to ensure that the Committee has access to the most recent performance results for the portfolio. Ideally, meetings will not be convened shortly after a quarter-end, as quarterly results are virtually irrelevant to the family's long-term investment performance and the family does not wish the Committee to focus on short-term events.

In an effort to avoid ad hoc decision-making and/or short-term thinking, the Committee will follow a seasonal schedule of meetings which will be conducted according to the agendas set forth below. Minutes will be taken of the decisions made at each meeting of the Committee.

First Triannual Meeting The first meeting of the Committee in each year will be convened after performance data is available for the prior calendar year. Ideally, this meeting will be scheduled before the end of the first quarter of the year. At the first meeting, the Committee will:

1. Review and approve the Minutes of the prior meeting of the Committee.
2. Review the performance for the prior year of the overall portfolio against the custom benchmark(s) established for the portfolio and, when possible, against the performance of similar investors.
3. Review the performance for the prior year of each manager engaged by the family against the benchmark established for that manager and, when possible, against the performance of similar managers.

4. Review the compliance of the family's investments with all guidelines set forth in the investment policy statement.
5. Review the compliance of each of the family's investment managers with the specific guidelines created for that manager.
6. Identify any performance issues with regard to any of the family's managers, such issues to be attended to before the next meeting of the Committee.

Second Triannual Meeting The second quarterly meeting of the Committee will be convened during mid-summer. The main purpose of the second meeting of the year is to ensure that the members of the Investment Committee continue to learn about the investment process and become ever more skillful at overseeing the family's portfolio. Thus, the agenda for the second meeting will be as follows:

1. Review and approve the Minutes of the prior meeting of the Committee.
2. Review (briefly) the year-to-date performance of the overall portfolio and the performance of individual managers, it being understood that partial year performance is far too short a period of time for meaningful data to be generated.
3. In the event that the Committee had identified concerns about the performance of any manager or managers at the first yearly meeting, that manager or those managers will be invited to attend the second quarterly meeting to discuss the issues with the Committee.
4. In the event that no manager performance issues were identified at the first yearly meeting, the purpose of the second meeting of the year (in addition to conducting a brief review of first quarter performance) will be to select an area of the investment process or the capital markets to examine in depth, generally with the assistance of an invited expert in the field. For example, the Committee may wish to examine a particular asset class, developments in portfolio design and asset allocation procedures, particular investment styles, the details of performance reporting and monitoring, macroeconomic issues, and so on.

Third Triannual Meeting The third quarterly meeting of the Committee will be convened in late fall or early winter. The main purpose of the third meeting of the year is to hear from managers who are active in a sector of the markets that is of interest to the family, but where the family is not currently invested. Thus, at each third meeting of the year, the Committee will:

1. Review and approve the Minutes of the prior meeting of the Committee.
2. Briefly review the year-to-date performance of the overall portfolio and the performance of individual managers.
3. Review the long-term (strategic) asset allocation strategy of the portfolio to determine whether or not changes in that strategy may be merited. Typically, such changes will be appropriate only if (a) there has been a substantial change in the objectives, risk tolerance, or makeup of the family, or (b) the Committee wishes to add or delete approved asset classes, usually as a result of studies undertaken at the third quarterly meeting.
4. Review the tactical asset allocation strategy of the portfolio to determine whether, in light of market conditions and, especially, pricing and valuation considerations, it may be in the family's interest to adjust its asset allocation posture tactically in the direction of assets that appear to be under-priced or where there otherwise appears to be relatively short-term opportunity in the markets. Except in rare circumstances, such tactical moves should not exceed the pre-set maximum or minimum exposures already established for each asset class.
5. Consider meeting with a manager or managers who are active in a sector of the markets that is of interest to the family but where the family is not currently invested.

Exhibit C

Spending Policy Statement
Smith Family
Adopted _____ 20__

Purpose of the Spending Policy Statement

The Smith family has adopted this Spending Policy Statement because the family is committed to the long-term preservation of its capital. We recognize that investment returns are uncertain and difficult to achieve. On the other hand, controlling our spending is entirely within our control.

The Function of the Family's Capital

The family's capital serves several important purposes:

1. The capital serves as a base of security in the event of any extraordinary threat to the future of the family, whether that threat arises from very negative events in the capital markets, from geopolitical changes that directly affect the family, or otherwise.

2. The capital supports the lifestyle of the family by making available a regular and predictable flow of funds to the various family unit budgets. Over long periods of time, it is important to preserve the purchasing power of the family and its members, thereby sustaining the family throughout the generations. Over-spending by current generations directly and negatively affects the ability of future generations of the family to enjoy lifestyles similar to those available today.

3. Support of the spending budget by the family's investment portfolio fosters the family's independence, shielding family members from outside influence by enabling them to generate internally a meaningful percentage of their spending. Allowing family members to chart their own course, without the specter of dependence on outside support, increases the freedom of family members and gives them the ability to pursue important activities that may not produce meaningful remuneration. The family values many professions that do not offer high income, including teaching, nursing, nonprofit work, law enforcement, military service, child care, and so on. As a family, we have been privileged to participate in these professions as we desired, and we wish to pass the same privilege on to our descendants. Ultimately, a family's human capital is more valuable than its financial capital.

4. As a family, we have always placed a high value on philanthropy. While it is true that current tax laws encourage charitable giving, even net of the tax effect, giving reduces the family's financial capital. Nonetheless, we have been fortunate to live in the US, a society that allowed us to profit from our hard work and our willingness to take risk. We have been fortunate in our genes and in the quality of our parenting. Many individuals are not so fortunate. While each generation of the family will decide for itself how best to focus its giving, broadly speaking it is the role of the family's philanthropy to increase opportunities for those who lack access to them and to improve the quality of life for all. Without possessing excess capital beyond what is needed to support the family's lifestyle, philanthropy would be impossible. This is another important reason why spending needs to be kept at responsible levels.

5. Finally, the family believes that the role of liquid capital is crucially important in maintaining and increasing the competitiveness of American society. Whether that capital is deployed in philanthropic giving, in support

for entrepreneurial activities, or in supplying the liquidity that is needed by businesses and financial institutions that are the backbone of the American and global economy, the prudent management and deployment of our capital is among the highest and best uses of our time and our talents.

The Need for Growth in the Family's Capital

Although the family is fortunate to possess a substantial fortune, that capital is under constant attack by inflation, taxation, poor investment markets, growth in the number of family members, and so on. If the family's portfolio does not grow, the ability of future generations of the family to spend at current levels will be curtailed. Just as we have benefited from the sound stewardship of prior generations of family members, it is now our job—and will soon be the job of our successors—to exercise sound stewardship in turn. Most of the headwinds our capital faces are beyond our control, but spending is not. All else being equal, the lower our spending today, the more capital the family will have tomorrow.

The Objectives of a Spending Policy

In a seminal article, Yale Professor and Nobel Laureate James Tobin wrote:

> The trustees of an endowed institution are the guardians of the future against the claims of the present. Their task is to preserve equity among generations. The trustees of an endowed university … assume the institution to be immortal. They want to know, therefore, the rate of [spending] from endowment which can be sustained indefinitely.
>
> Consuming endowment income so defined means in principle that the existing endowment can continue to support the same set of activities that it is now supporting. This rule says that the current consumption should not benefit from the prospect of future gifts to endowment. Sustained consumption rises to encompass and enlarge the scope of activities when, but not before, capital gifts enlarge the endowment.

Although Professor Tobin was addressing spending by an endowed institution, his argument applies even more directly to spending by an "endowed" family. Our family was endowed by earlier generations who accomplished extraordinary things and created the wealth whose management we now oversee. Unlike an endowed institution, however, as a family we are unlikely ever to receive additional "gifts." The capital we have created as a family is probably all the capital we will ever have.

Therefore, we must spend as a current generation at levels that are consistent with our investment returns and which will not diminish the family's future wealth. Too much current spending will cause future family wealth to fall, harming our grandchildren and their descendants.

Any family spending policy should thus be designed to meet two competing objectives. The first objective is to release current income to the family budget in a stable, predictable stream, since large fluctuations are difficult to accommodate through changes in the family's lifestyle. The second objective is to protect the value of the family's assets against inflation, allowing spending to be supported at today's level far into the future.

The Family Spending Rule

The family's investment objective, as specified in the family's investment policy statement, is to preserve, and to the extent consistent with this primary objective to enhance, the inflation-adjusted value of our family's assets, net of spending. Therefore, apart from the purchase of a personal residence, targeted annual spending by family members from their investment assets, exclusive of taxes and investment expenses, will not exceed [x]% annually.

Exhibit D

Manager Guideline
XYC Municipal Short-Term Bond Portfolio
Adopted _____ 20__

Purpose

The investment objectives and guidelines described below will govern the investment management of the assets of the Client for this Municipal Short-Term Bond Portfolio. Any strategy or action that differs from, or is inconsistent with, the objectives and guidelines contained in this document will require advance discussion with the Client Advisor and prior written approval by the Client.

Objectives and Portfolio

The strategy is focused on holding bonds with generally higher credit quality than the benchmark, but with an effective duration range that typically falls within a band to the benchmark effective duration. The product is actively managed, with performance measured relative to the Merrill Lynch 1–2 Year Index.

Guidelines

Subject to the following guidelines, the Portfolio Manager has full discretion in investment decisions. The Portfolio Manager, however, shall undertake no action that can reasonably be deemed to be inconsistent with these guidelines.

Allowable Securities

The manager is expected to invest primarily in fixed income securities issued by US municipalities and other US tax-exempt organizations. The use of commingled funds including mutual funds, other than for the investment of temporary cash balances, is not allowed unless pre-approved by the Client.

Diversification and Credit Quality Guidelines

The portfolio will:

- At the time of purchase, have a minimum short-term debt rating of money market instruments or other instruments having a maturity of less than 1 year, of A1/P1. The minimum long-term debt rating (or parity security rating) for all other instruments is Baa3 or above as rated by Moody's Investors Service, Inc., or equivalently rated by S&P, Fitch, Inc., or another Nationally Recognized Statistical Rating Organization ("NRSRO"). If a security is split-rated, the higher rating shall apply. Further, if an issue is downgraded below these minimums, the manager will determine the appropriate action (sell or hold) based on the perceived risk and expected return.
- Limit investment in securities of any individual non-state obligors to no more than 5% of the portfolio at the time of purchase.

Portfolio Duration

The Manager will generally maintain an effective duration for the portfolio varying between 60% and 110% of the effective duration of the benchmark. Notwithstanding the above, there may be periods during the year the portfolio could be outside the above referenced effective duration band due to the normal effects of the reinvestment of securities. The maximum effective duration of any individual security held within the portfolio shall not exceed 3 years.

Cash Equivalent Investments

This portfolio should remain as fully invested as practical once the account becomes fully funded. Normally, cash balances will be held to less than 10% of the value of the portfolio. Cash in the account will be swept into a custodial tax-exempt money market instrument specified by the Client.

Derivatives

The use of options, futures, or other derivatives in the portfolio is prohibited without the prior written consent of the Client.

Leverage

Explicit use of leverage in the portfolio will not be allowed without prior notification to the Client Advisor and written consent of the Client. Leverage is herein defined as a situation in which the portfolio as a whole is more than 100% invested in the securities permitted by these guidelines.

Temporary, Emergency, or Defensive Investments

The Manager may, in its discretion, invest portfolio assets in liquid short-term US Treasury securities not meeting these guidelines only for temporary (e.g. start-up), emergency, or defensive purposes.

Contributions and Withdrawals

Interest and dividends generated by the portfolio will be reinvested in the portfolio unless otherwise directed by the Client.

Additional contributions or withdrawals may be directed from time to time at the discretion of the Client. No withdrawals can be made from the Portfolio unless authorized in writing, via letter and/or e-mail, and followed by verbal authorization by the Client.

Review and Modification

These investment objectives and guidelines shall be reviewed periodically by the Client Advisor with the Portfolio Manager, at a minimum annually, and revised or confirmed as appropriate.

Any changes to the investment objectives and guidelines deemed necessary by the Portfolio Manager or the Client will be promptly communicated by the Portfolio Manager to the Client Advisor and subsequently agreed upon and confirmed in writing by the Client and the Portfolio Manager.

Performance Measurement and Reporting

1. The portfolio's total return will be reported by the Manager to the Client and the Client Advisor on a monthly basis.
2. The Portfolio Manager will provide the Client and the Client Advisor with quarterly written investment reports that document holdings and transactions and that discuss:

   - Account structure versus requirements
   - Past asset performance and investment strategy
   - Anticipated future strategy

3. The Portfolio Manager will keep the Client and the Client Advisor informed as to material changes, if any, in its organization, ownership, financial condition, investment personnel, investment philosophy, or decision-making process. Additionally, the Portfolio Manager will be responsible for communicating to the Client and the Client Advisor, all significant changes in investment outlook, portfolio strategy, and allocation of account assets.

4. The Client will keep the Portfolio Manager informed as to any material changes in its plan(s), including changes in requirements or restrictions that might affect the Portfolio Manager's ability to fulfill its investment management assignment.
5. The Portfolio Manager shall not be responsible for providing economic or interest rate forecasts.
6. The Portfolio Manager will initiate oral communication with the Client and the Client Advisor whenever unusual events occur that have the potential to significantly affect the portfolio.
7. Communications from the Portfolio Manager will be directed to the following individuals (see Approval, below).

Approval

The foregoing guidelines are approved as of the day and year first written above.

_____   _____

On behalf of the Client   Title

_____   _____

On behalf of the Portfolio Manager   Title

_____   _____

On behalf of the Client Advisor   Title

7

Evaluating Money Managers
for Family Portfolios

Many financial professionals are used to working mostly with mutual funds, index funds, and ETFs. While these kinds of products can be perfectly appropriate for ultra-wealthy families, you will not be able to get by on such products alone. Instead, you will need to be in a position to recommend separate account managers, hedge funds, and venture capital and private equity funds.

Why separate account managers? The main reasons have to do with taxes (see the discussion below), although many separate account fees are also lower than the mutual fund or commingled version of the product.

Why hedge funds? Partly because of the shift of money management talent away from long-only management and into hedge funds. In addition, hedge funds allow managers to utilize more strategies—short-selling, using leverage, and so on. During tricky market environments without dominant directionality, and during poor markets, hedge funds can preserve capital. Finally, non-directional hedge funds can serve as a useful and often higher-returning alternative to fixed income.

And what about private equity (PE), including both venture capital (VC) and private real estate? Unlike smaller investors, ultra-wealthy families can often get access to the top PE and VC funds, as well as the best real estate managers. In those worlds there is a huge difference between the top-performing managers and the average-performing managers. Also, these kinds of products often significantly outperform the long markets while offering deferred long-term capital gains tax treatment.

© The Author(s) 2020
G. Curtis, *Advising the Ultra-Wealthy*, https://doi.org/10.1007/978-3-030-57605-9_7

A full description of the process of finding, diligencing, and monitoring money managers is beyond the scope of this book.[1] But since these skills will be necessary for you to remain competitive in the wealth management sector, we will go over some of the key challenges.

Finding Top Managers

Competitive wealth management firms locate top money managers mainly via their own experience and contacts. Suppose, for example, the firm wants to find a good high-yield bond manager. Most likely, the firm will query its existing stable of fixed-income managers and ask them who is especially capable in the high yield space, who their toughest competitors are. The firm might or might not end up with one of the managers on that list, but it's a very good place to start.

But if you are new to the ultra-wealthy world you likely have no experience and few contacts. Given that, here are few strategies to consider:

- Start with the firms you are already working with. If you are using a bond mutual fund or ETF you like, it's very possible that the same firm offers a separate account version of a high-yield product.
- Invest in a database of asset managers. There are several good databases available and most are searchable. No good wealth management firm will actually use a database to select a manager, but if you are new to the business, you have to start somewhere. In any event, the database can be used to compare the performance of many managers in the same asset category against the manager you are considering.
- Attend conferences at which money managers present. You can not only listen to the presentations, but very often you will have the opportunity to speak directly to managers that interest you.
- Ask around. Although wealth managers are intensely competitive, if you are just starting out, most other wealth management firms won't view you as a dangerous competitor and they may be happy to share the name of a good manager with you. (Unless, of course, the manager is capacity-constrained.)
- Serve on investment committees. If you join the boards of larger nonprofit organizations—or your own college, for example—you will learn a great deal about the managers those institutions are using. Some of these organi-

---

[1] For more detail, see Gregory Curtis, *The Stewardship of Wealth* (Wiley 2013), especially Chap. 20.

zations will also use investment consultants, and those firms can be a rich source of manager ideas. Keep in mind, however, that many managers that make perfect sense for institutional investors will have tax characteristics that make them problematic for taxable families.

Conducting Diligence on Separate Account Managers

If you are used to dealing with mutual funds and ETFs, attempting to perform diligence on a separate account manager might seem challenging. But here is a checklist of issues you should look into:

- Tax flexibility. One of the main reasons for using separate account managers is tax flexibility. Therefore you will need to be sure that the managers you are considering are actually tax-friendly. When they are selling securities, are they conscious of long- versus short-term gains? Are they paying attention to tax lots and even allow you and your clients to designate which tax lots are to be sold? These and similar questions need to be looked into.
- Investment philosophy. Probably the most important issue to focus on is the manager's investment philosophy, because that bears directly on the manager's ability to outperform. Unfortunately, any manager who has been in business for a while will be able to talk a good game. As you gain experience interviewing managers, you will get better at separating the pepper from the, uh, fly droppings.
- Investment discipline. You will want to determine whether the manager is a disciplined investor, that is, whether it sticks to its investment philosophy in good times and bad. The only way to do this effectively is to conduct a detailed review of the manager's performance during periods when the wind has been at its back and when the wind has been in its face. Attribution analysis and a close examination of investment decisions that turned out badly can shed important light on these questions. Of particular importance is the managers' "sell discipline"—the managers' rules that determine when a security is to be sold. Sell discipline is important because otherwise managers will tend to hold appreciated securities far too long and to believe that they are "smarter than the market."
- Experience. Any manager can outperform over a short period of time. As you know from picking mutual funds and ETFs, investors who buy funds after a period of outperformance will usually be disappointed because fund/manager performance tends to revert toward the mean. Ideally, a

manager's performance should be observed over a full market cycle, that is, a period of time during which the manager's investment style and philosophy are in vogue as well as a period of time when they are out of fashion.

- Asset base. Some investment styles can be carried on at huge scale (high-quality bonds, for example), but others will be successful only if they remain niche businesses. Indeed, scale can also matter in bond management because trading costs, especially the costs of trading municipal bonds, can eat up a large fraction of the potential returns. But small cap managers face the opposite problem: the float of small cap stocks can be very thin, making it difficult to buy or sell even a few hundreds of millions of dollars of a stock without moving the price.
- Alignment of interests. Like any business, money managers attempt to maximize their profits. If those profits can only be maximized by acting in the interests of clients, the relationship is likely to be satisfactory. Unfortunately, there are many ways in which money managers can increase their profits at the expense of client investment returns. One obvious example is for the manager to emphasize asset gathering over returns. Alignment between manager and client will never be perfect, but the closer that alignment is, the happier you and your clients will be.
- Organizational stability. A sound investment philosophy can only be implemented by an investment team that has worked together for years and that has experienced little turnover, especially at the top of the organization. Organizational instability—including the sale of the firm—is an excellent warning sign that performance is likely to deteriorate.
- Quality of the client base. This may seem an odd issue, but the quality of a manager's client base can make an important difference in the manager's ability to function with minimal interference and maximum stability. Typically, managers whose recent performance has been outstanding will often wind up with a lot of "hot money," that is, clients who will pull out at the first sign of underperformance.
- Personal integrity. This should go without saying. While it may seem harsh, any blemishes on a manager's record should disqualify the firm from serious consideration. This includes regulatory problems at the firm level and also personal problems at the individual level. If you have the slightest doubt about a manager's integrity, either run a background check or run the other way.

In addition to looking for positive data, you should also be on the lookout for objectionable characteristics: a focus on asset gathering, a weak back office, a history of regulatory problems, an organization that is primarily engaged in activities other than money management, and so on. The presence of even one of these characteristics should raise a question in your mind.

Before meeting with the manager—preferably in its own office—you will want to obtain the manager's pitch book and Form ADV, you will want to search the Web for relevant information about the manager, and you will want to prepare style-based return attribution analyses.

Monitoring Best-in-Class Managers

Once approved, you should monitor approved managers' continuing quality in several ways. First, generate a report that measures the difference between each manager's monthly return and its relevant benchmark (this difference is referred to as "tracking error"). Then compare that month's tracking error to the manager's 5-year historical tracking error. To the extent that a manager's tracking error in any given month is ±1 standard deviation away from its historical tracking error, you should initiate a call to the manager. During these calls, ask them to describe what factor(s) caused them to perform unusually well or unusually poorly that month. Their responses should be recorded in your database. Simply as a result of this monthly review process, you will, on average, speak to your managers three times per year. You should also formally re-evaluate each approved manager on roughly an annual basis in order to re-affirm your confidence in them.

Second, when one of your managers experiences a change of control, acquires another firm, or suffers the loss of a key portfolio manager, you should promptly seek to understand how these changes may affect the manager.

Managers should rarely be terminated for poor performance alone. Instead, you should terminate managers when you conclude that they no longer maintain the differential advantages that caused you to hire them in the first place. Examples of such reasons might include:

- Departure of a critical investment professional
- Significant style drift
- Failure to limit asset growth to levels promised
- Failure to communicate or be responsive to requests for information

Alternative Asset Managers

Hedge Funds A hedge fund manager is a manager only more so—a manager on steroids, if you will. Everything said above about managers in general goes for hedge fund managers, but they are all even more critical. Long-only managers can underperform, sometimes substantially, but they rarely blow up and lose all an investor's capital. Hedge funds do this quite regularly.

The fundamental concern about hedge funds is that the assets managed by hedge fund managers are not held in custody in the usual sense of the word. When an investor engages a long-only manager, the manager never actually gains control of the investor's cash or securities. Cash and securities remain in the hands of a bank or brokerage firm that is acting as the asset custodian for the investor. The portfolio manager has, in reality or in effect, a limited power of attorney to direct the investments in the account. The manager can cause the account to sell GE and buy Microsoft. But the GE stock doesn't leave the custodian's hands until the proceeds from its sale arrive, and the funds required to buy Microsoft don't leave the custodian's hands until the Microsoft stock arrives. (All this occurs electronically, of course, and is subject to the prevailing settlement rules.)

But when an investor engages a hedge fund manager, the cash and securities are held in accounts controlled by the hedge fund, not the investor. Typically, the cash and securities are held by a so-called prime broker for the hedge fund. But whereas in a traditional custody arrangement the investor is the custodian's client, in a prime brokerage arrangement the *hedge fund* is the broker's customer. The prime broker's loyalties—to say nothing of his lucrative business dealings—lie exclusively with the hedge fund. If the hedge fund manager wakes up some morning with a hankering to go to Brazil, he can simply wire all the funds in the hedge fund account to his private account in Sao Paulo and hop on the next plane.

PE, Venture, and Real Estate Managers As noted above, the key challenge with these investments is getting access to the best managers. Until you have been in the ultra-wealthy advisory business for a long time, the best way to get access is likely to be via funds of funds.

The fund of funds business has been in the doldrums for years because few advisors or their clients like paying the double layer of fees. And, indeed, most funds of funds aren't worth the extra cost. But a few funds of funds are worth their fees and these can play an important role in your client portfolios until you can build up enough credibility to gain access to the best funds directly.

(Note that this is unlikely ever to happen with the very top-tier venture funds because they are always massively over-subscribed.)

Diligencing PE, venture, and private real estate funds is complex. It involves examining not merely their track records but also many other issues. For example, where does their deal flow come from and how likely is it to continue? How stable is the general partnership that manages the fund? How stable is the investor base? Is fund size getting out of control? Is the GP sticking to its knitting or is it expanding into other sectors where its experience is limited?

Ongoing diligence is also important, because eventually the GP will be raising another fund and you will have to decide whether to "re-up." Thus, the same questions (above) that you ask before investing in the first fund will need to be asked again before you decide whether or not to invest in the next fund.

Conclusion

Building a manager research effort that is worthy of an ultra-wealthy client base is one of the most complicated and expensive aspects of competing for the business of those families. It doesn't have to happen overnight, of course—you can build your capabilities over time. But if you expect to be competitive in the ultra-wealthy client space, a sound manager research group is a must.

8

On Governance: Decision-Making in Families

When the family still owned its company, that company came with a predesigned governance structure: shareholders (that is, the family) elected a board of directors, the board engaged a management team, and the management team had a hierarchy with a CEO at the top. But once the company was sold that governance structure went away. What will replace it?

As the family's financial advisor you will be mainly concerned with how the family makes investment decisions. But the family itself will need to make decisions in many other areas as well.

Every family will organize itself differently, but typically, a family governance structure will include some or all of the following features:

- The family's family office will typically be governed by a board consisting of both family members and close advisors.
- Apart from the family office, many families will also have a family board or family council elected by the family members.
- Most ultra-wealthy families will have annual family meetings to which all family members will be invited.
- A family will typically establish an investment committee that may include both family and non-family members. The committee may have final say over investment decisions or it may be advisory in nature, with final decisions made by the family.
- However a family structures itself, there will typically be a family constitution setting out the various governance features and how family members and advisors are to be elected to serve.

© The Author(s) 2020
G. Curtis, *Advising the Ultra-Wealthy*, https://doi.org/10.1007/978-3-030-57605-9_8

Family Investment Committees

Especially when family members aren't experienced investors—as is usually the case—a family investment committee can play an important role in helping the family make sensible decisions and to feel more comfortable making those decisions. The committee will likely consist of both family members and trusted advisors—who need not be investment professionals—and the committee may be the final decision maker or may simply make recommendations to the family.

It is important that a family investment committee be carefully structured and populated, because investment committees tend to suffer all the usual problems associated with "decision making by committee." In other words, decisions can be made far too slowly, and decisions can sometimes represent an unfortunate compromise—often the lowest-common-denominator.

The Family Foundation

All too often the family charitable foundation exists outside the family's governance structure. A foundation isn't technically owned by the family—instead, its assets have been permanently dedicated to charity and can't legally be used to benefit the family. Fearful of IRS oversight, many families keep the foundation at arm's length. The family may control the foundation's board, but that board and the foundation's charitable activities aren't integrated into the family's governance.

This is usually a mistake, because a foundation can be a very useful tool for educating younger family members in governance, philanthropy, obligations to the broader community, and so on. There are various ways to move the foundation closer to the family. For example, the members of the foundation's governing board can rotate on and off the board over time, with nominees provided by the family council. The foundation can create a "junior" board that has the ability to recommend small grants and serves as a training ground for future trustees.

The Root family, famous for inventing the iconic Coca-Cola bottle, has developed an online tool that allows interested family members to comment on proposals the family foundation has received and even to suggest possible grantmaking opportunities that fall within the foundation's philanthropic priorities.

Private Trust Companies

Private trust companies (PTCs), sometimes referred to as "family trust companies," have become quite popular in recent years. While the subject of PTCs goes well beyond this chapter, if you work with the ultra-wealthy long enough you will encounter PTCs.

A PTC is a special kind of trust company that is established to serve only one family. Many years ago a few wealthy families established forerunners of PTCs that eventually evolved into commercial trust companies serving a broader public. The Smith family in Chicago, for example, established Northern Trust Company, the Phipps family set up Bessemer Trust Company, and four wealthy families combined to establish the United States Trust Company.

Today, several states are competing for PTC business, offering laws that are tax- and regulatory-friendly. These include South Dakota, Nevada, Wyoming, Delaware, Alaska, and Ohio. All the PTC laws are slightly different, and so families need to be very well-advised before selecting a specific jurisdiction. Assuming the tax and regulatory issues are similar, families will normally select the jurisdiction that is easiest for them to travel to—most states require that at least one meeting per year be held in the state, and some states require that all important decisions be taken in the state. There are also offshore jurisdictions that cater to PTCs: the Cayman Islands, Bermuda, Hong Kong, and Singapore.

Family governance is one of the leading reasons families set up PTCs. As the generations come along and family members become both more numerous and less connected to each other, a PTC can serve as a venue for meeting, talking, connecting, and dealing with longer term wealth-preservation issues.

PTCs also circumvent the problem of trustee succession since it is the PTC itself that is the fiduciary. Many families will find that finding individuals who are both willing and able to function as a trustee becomes extremely difficult over the decades.

PTCs do come with some disadvantages. Cost, for example, may make establishing and maintaining a PTC prohibitive for families with less than $100 million. PTCs also add a layer of complexity to a family's operations, slowing down decision-making.

Perhaps the biggest disadvantage of PTCs is the very perpetual nature of the entity. For all its tax and governance advantages, PTCs can infantilize future generations, who may come to see themselves as uninvolved in the family's wealth. They are simply trust fund beneficiaries who receive checks from some mysterious source every quarter.

9

Family Philanthropy

Most American families will want to find ways to "give back" to their communities and to society at large, recognizing their good fortune in living in a society that encourages wealth creation. Ultra-wealthy families in particular often have well-organized, well-thought-out philanthropic programs that have been in place for many years, if not for many generations.

Newly wealthy families, however, often struggle to get their minds around how best to give back, and as their financial advisor you may be one of the people they turn to for advice.

Organizing a successful family philanthropic program involves two main areas of inquiry: what philanthropic vehicles are most appropriate and how best to settle on the family's philanthropic priorities.

Charitable Vehicles

Vehicles through which families carry out their charitable programs typically include one or more of the following:

Private foundations. For larger philanthropic programs, a private foundation will usually be the best choice. And I mean *large*—if a family's foundation will have less than about $25 million in assets, and isn't expected to grow much, a donor-advised fund (DAF) is probably a better option (see the discussion below).

© The Author(s) 2020
G. Curtis, *Advising the Ultra-Wealthy*, https://doi.org/10.1007/978-3-030-57605-9_9

A thorough discussion of the operation of charitable foundations is beyond the scope of this book, but there are several issues a financial advisor to wealthy families and their foundations should understand. For example:

- High spending requirements. Foundations must give to charity approximately 5% of their assets every year, calculated on a rolling 3-year basis. Although foundations pay only a small (1% or 2%) excise tax, this is still a very high spending rate. Needless to say, the high required spending will need to be taken into account in designing the foundation's overall strategy. In addition, however, foundations that are intended to be permanent charitable vehicles should be encouraged to exercise spending discipline. Difficult as it will sometimes be, a well-managed foundation will give away *exactly* 5%, not 5.5% or even higher, as many foundations do. The reality is that most foundations are gradually liquidating themselves in real terms.
- Self-dealing. The IRS requires that foundations operate for the public good, not for the benefit of private persons, and especially not for the benefit of individuals closely connected to the foundation (known as "disqualified persons"). Thus, if a family member makes a personal pledge to a charity, the family foundation cannot pay the pledge. Similarly, if the family's foundation has its offices in the family office, the family will need to take very special care if rent is being charged to the foundation.
- Foundation advisory fees. Related to the self-dealing rules, if you are advising both the family and the foundation it is very important that you structure your fee arrangements properly. Suppose, for example, that the family's assets are $200 million and the foundation's assets are $50 million. By aggregating the assets of both entities, both will pay a lower basis point fee and you may imagine that you have thereby helped both the family and its foundation. In fact, the IRS could—and probably will—take the position that the family's fee was reduced because of the assets of the foundation, and therefore a self-dealing violation has occurred. This sort of error will not endear you to the family.
- Control. History is replete with examples of families who lost control of their foundations and soon found that the money they earned was being used to support causes they disagreed with: consider Ford, MacArthur, and so on. Foundation governing boards are self-perpetuating, and it is therefore extremely important that families allow board members (or trustees) to serve only if the family has complete confidence in those individuals.

- Regulatory hell. In addition to the issues already discussed, there are many exacting rules and regulations governing private foundations, so many that you may spend as much time with lawyers and accountants as you do with prospective grantees. And it will only get worse. Beginning with the Tax Reform Act of 1986, Congress has been—and is increasingly—hostile to private foundations, which are viewed by many Congressional Representatives as unaccountable pools of dark and mysterious capital. This is yet another reason to avoid private foundations unless the asset base is very large.

Donor-advised funds. A donor-advised fund (DAF) is a vehicle through which families can set up charitable funds with far less operating and regulatory complexity. Typically, a DAF will be established by a public charity such as a community foundation.[1] Instead of setting up the Smith Family Foundation as a stand-alone private foundation, the family could establish the Smith Family Fund as a DAF at its local community foundation. Here are some key features to be aware of regarding DAFs:

- A DAF is usually a better idea than a foundation for smaller giving programs.
- Unlike private foundations, community foundations must raise funds every year in order to maintain their public charity status. To encourage affluent families to set up DAFs, many community foundations will allow a family to keep its existing advisor—you—even though the funds have moved to the DAF.
- Among the advantages of DAFs are (a) there is no 5% annual giving requirement and (b) grants made by the DAF can be made anonymously, since they will appear to be coming from the organization where the DAF resides.
- Among the disadvantages of DAFs is that the donors aren't, at the end of the day, in complete control of their giving. Technically, donors of DAFs are merely making *recommendations* to the parent organization (the community foundation, for example). It's certainly true that the parent will almost always approve a donor's recommendation—otherwise, people would stop establishing DAFs at the parent. But particularly controversial gifts, or gifts that might possibly be construed as improper (gifts to individuals, foreign organizations, or other private foundations), might be disapproved.

---

[1] DAFs are also offered by private financial firms: Vanguard, Fidelity, Schwab, and others.

- As time goes by and subsequent generations multiply, move away or otherwise lose interest in the DAF, the corpus can revert to the parent organization, where it might be used in ways unpalatable to the original donors. If your client is worried about this eventuality the founding documents of the DAF can specify what ultimately happens to the corpus.

Personal giving. Whether or not a family maintains a foundation or donor-advised fund, most family members will also have personal giving programs. Often, the most efficient way to give personally will be to gift appreciated securities. If a family member sold $100,000 worth of stock with a cost basis of $50,000, federal and state capital gains taxes could easily eat up $12,000 of the gain, resulting in only $88,000 available for gifting. But by simply donating the $100,000 worth of stock, the family member will make a larger gift and get a $100,000 tax deduction.

Designing a Family Philanthropic Program

It is highly unlikely that a family will ask your advice about *who* they should be giving their charitable money to. On the other hand, they may well seek your advice about *how* to establish a successful philanthropy program. By "successful" a family will typically mean (a) the giving program makes an appropriate impact and (b) the program is meaningful to the family.

Keep in mind that, unless your fee structure allows you to charge specifically for the time you devote to philanthropic discussions with the family, this sort of thing can turn into a time sink and destroy the profitability of the relationship. The best way to handle this kind of request for help is to proceed far enough so that you understand what the family needs and then bring in an expert who specializes in the field.

One bit of advice the family might need is to determine how to set its giving priorities, especially in a situation where different family members, family units, and family generations may have different points of view. In such a case the best way forward is likely to use a specialist who can work with the family to allow all points of view to be heard while still focusing in on a few areas where the family's giving can make an impact.

Note that in a particularly diverse family it might be useful to have a series of main giving priorities while still allowing grants to be made outside these focus areas in order to acknowledge the opinions of other family members.

In addition to the question of which causes to support, a foundation needs to consider what *types* of grants it wishes to give. Some foundations will want to be extremely activist in their giving, disrupting the status quo, while others will focus more on preserving what is already good and valuable in the society.

Also, some foundations will wish to focus on giving general operating support, feeling that the nonprofit organization itself is the best judge of how to spend the money. Other foundations will focus on giving support for specific projects, thus giving themselves greater control over how the money is used.

Using the Foundation as an Investment Training Vehicle

One big issue for families is how to train rising generations to handle investment issues. Young people are busy and typically not much interested in learning how to invest. But most young people love giving money away.

Thus, many families will use the lure of being a philanthropist to entice younger family members to attend foundation meetings—where, importantly, they will have to sit through the investment discussions. In fact, some families create informal "junior boards" that allow rising generations to attend foundation meetings, offer their opinions about grantmaking, and, in some cases, actually decide on smaller grants.

These junior boards do help train younger family members in the art of philanthropy, but they also force young people to sit through investment presentations. In some families, junior board members cannot expect to graduate to the "big board" unless they have demonstrated mastery not merely of giving but also of investing. After all, if the investment side of things is neglected, there won't be much money to give away.

Integrating the Foundation into the Family

Because of the self-dealing rules that apply to private foundations, many families end up with a foundation that sits off to the side of the family as a kind of odd appendage. This is an overreaction to the regulatory requirements, and as the family's financial advisor, you can perform a service by offering ideas for integrating the foundation more fully into the family's other activities. For example:

- Integrate the foundation with the family office. The family will need to be well-advised if they plan to charge the foundation for office space, supplies, administrative support, and so on, but these issues can be overcome.
- Convene the foundation trustee (or director) meetings in the same spaces where the family's board meets.
- Establish one investment committee to oversee both the family's personal capital and the foundation's endowment. If this is done, it might be prudent for the investment committee simply to make *recommendations* to the foundation trustees.
- Establish a training program for prospective foundation trustees that is integrated with the family's broader training programs for younger family members.
- Establish a mechanism, probably online, whereby family members who aren't trustees of the foundation can weigh in on grant requests, suggest possible grantees or giving programs, and so on.

10

They're Selling the Family Company: Now What?

Many families who have been superb operators of a business are nonetheless completely flummoxed when it comes to dealing with liquid capital—after all, it's a profoundly different world. Although before the sale the family's wealth was highly concentrated into one security, it was a security the family was comfortable with. After all, they knew the business very well, understood the industry, the competition, the suppliers, the customers, and the workforce. Now, suddenly, they have to invest in securities and markets they can't control and don't understand.

But the fact is that thousands of families have navigated the new world of liquid wealth and have managed to preserve and grow their capital for generations. Your client can too.

Every family is different of course, but in this chapter, I walk through the ten steps a family should take as soon as it becomes clear that the family business will be sold—even before the closing.

Step One

Read Chap. 11—"What Is the Wealth For?" This is the single most important step a family can take as it sells its business.

© The Author(s) 2020
G. Curtis, *Advising the Ultra-Wealthy*, https://doi.org/10.1007/978-3-030-57605-9_10

Step Two

Implement a Sound Governance and Decision-Making System If the family's investment decision-making will be handled by the matriarch and patriarch, that may seem like a simple situation. But unless Mom and Dad are experienced investment people, they will likely find it difficult to respond to your (sometimes quite complex) recommendations. In any event, as the generations go by, many more people will be—or will *want* to be—involved in decision-making.

For most families, therefore, it will make sense to establish an investment committee. The committee need not consist of investment professionals, although a few experienced investors will be a plus. What is needed are people of sound judgment and who the family trusts.

In addition to an investment committee, many families will have a family council or assembly, a family board, and various family committees. Large families should also consider organizing a private trust company (PTC), sometimes called a "family trust company." PTCs arose to deal with the perplexing problem of having to find trustees for the family's many trusts. Find individuals to serve? Hire a bank trust department?

The PTC can serve as the family's go-to fiduciary, and because PTCs are usually incorporated in states that have abolished the rule against perpetuities, PTCs can last, theoretically at least, forever.

Part of your job as the family's financial advisor is to help guide the family through the many governance issues they face. You might also wish to introduce the family to family governance experts. For more information, see Chap. 8, "On Governance—Decision-Making in Families."

Step Three

Engage a Good Financial Advisor Hopefully, this is you. But if you find yourself pitching against other prospective advisors, remind the family that a good advisor is one who is (a) free of conflicts of interest and (b) deeply experienced in advising ultra-wealthy families. They should avoid large firms (to whom they won't be an important client) and firms that focus on institutional clients such as universities and pension plans.

The reason for avoiding institutionally oriented advisory firms is that families have a very different relationship with their capital than institutions do.

Consider how long and hard the family has worked to make its money. Institutions, by contrast, have money handed to them on a silver platter—mainly by families!

In addition, consider what happens if an institutional investor does a poor investment job and loses a great deal of its capital—as happened to many institutions during the Global Financial Crisis. They simply launch a capital campaign and raise more money. But try that as a family. For this reason, families tend to be capital preservation-oriented in their investment outlook while institutions are not.

Finally, institutions are *relative* return investors, while families are *absolute* return investors. To take an extreme example, suppose that University A has just lost 25% of its endowment in a market downturn, while its peer institutions lost 26%. University A is happy—it outperformed its peers. But I have yet to meet a family who would be happy if it lost a quarter of its wealth.

A good advisor—like you—who is focused on working with families will be able to evolve along with the family. As the family becomes more experienced with the world of liquid wealth, you will be able to make more complex recommendations.

Finally, good family investment advisors aren't just hired guns. A family's relationships with its custodian, money managers, and performance reporting vendors will likely be purely arm's length and commercial. But the family's relationship with its investment advisor—you—should be different. You should become a trusted counsellor to the family and, ultimately, a friend.

Step Four

Find a Good Asset Custodian As you know, asset custody will form the base on which all else is built. A custodian—typically a very large bank—safeguards investment assets by holding them in a segregated account owned by the investor. The fact that the account is "segregated" is important—it means that the investor's assets are formally separated from the assets of the custodian. In the unlikely event that the bank should go bankrupt, the investor's assets will not be subject to the claims of the bank's creditors.

This is not the case, it is important to note, with brokerage firms that are acting as a custodian. If the broker goes under, the investor's assets go with it. For this reason, all brokerage firms carry large amounts of insurance, designed to protect investors against just this possibility (remember Lehman Brothers). Unfortunately, one has to wonder whether the insurance firms themselves could survive the bankruptcy of a major brokerage house.

Surprising numbers of investors don't bother to have their assets held safely in a custody arrangement, but simply place the assets at the disposal of whoever is managing the money. In such a case, they are placing themselves entirely at the mercy of the honesty of the money management firm and all its employees, a very foolish thing to do.

In essence, a custodian holds and reports on all the client's investment assets, including cash and securities. Money managers (see Chap. 7, "Evaluating Money Managers for Family Portfolios") engaged by a family will be given a limited power of attorney to direct the investment of the funds assigned to that manager (the custodian will set up separate accounts for each manager), but those managers will not have access to the cash or securities in the account.

Certain types of accounts are inherently not subject to actual custody and are reported by the custodian only as line-item entries. Typical examples include mutual funds (each mutual fund has its own custodian), hedge funds (which are "custodied," in a very limited sense, by a prime broker), and private equity funds.

It is easy to identify the few financial institutions that aspire to excellence in the custody business. This is because asset custody is an extremely capital-intensive business, requiring massive and ongoing investments in technology and personnel merely to stay even with the competition. At the same time, custody is largely a commodity business with low profit margins. This unhappy combination of massive investment and low profits means that, globally, there are only a relative handful of institutions that have chosen to compete in this business.

However, once the small group of best-in-class custodians has been identified, it is more difficult to select the most appropriate custodian for your particular needs. At bottom, the decision comes down to extensive day-by-day experience with the performance of individual custodians handling different kinds of clients and assets. Most families will find it best to rely on your guidance regarding the best custodians.

Master custodians are discussed in more detail in Chap. 15.

Step Five

Design a Long-Term Investment Strategy The single most important determinant of a family's long-term investment outcomes is whether or not a family, working with you, has developed an investment strategy *that is right for that family*. The strategy followed by Yale has worked well for Yale, but it won't work well for the family (or for anyone else who doesn't employ Yale's Chief Investment Officer, David Swensen).

An investment strategy, at its highest level, articulates how much risk a family is willing to take and where those risks will be taken. A simple strategy, for example, might be to put 60% of the capital in stocks and 40% in bonds. A more aggressive strategy might be 70%/30%, and a more conservative strategy might be 50%/50%.

But which stocks? US stocks, international stocks, emerging markets stocks? What about small company stocks in the US and abroad? What about hedge funds, private equity, and real estate?

And which bonds? Municipal bonds, certainly, but should the portfolio be concentrated in your state of residence, giving you a double tax advantage, or should the portfolio be diversified nationally? What about high-yield bonds or cash?

All these and many more issues should be dealt with in the family's investment policy statement (see Step Eight, below). For more information, see Chap. 14, in the section titled "Asset Allocation for Ultra-Wealthy Families," the "Designing Portfolios for Ultra-Wealthy Families."

Step Six

Select Money Managers A typical portfolio for a wealthy family will have somewhere between 15 and 40 investment managers. Each manager will manage a specific portion of the portfolio. For example, if the family chooses to use passive management for its US equity exposure, the manager might be the Vanguard S&P 500 Index Fund. If the family chooses to a manager employing artificial intelligence (AI) systems, it might hire a hedge fund that selects securities using AI, computer-driven methods. If a family chooses to invest in venture capital, it will become a limited partner in a venture capital fund or funds of funds.

All of these decisions will be driven by you, of course. Identifying, evaluating, and monitoring money managers is a highly specialized activity and almost all families will rely on their advisor to handle this part of the investment process. However, larger families might engage an investment professional to work inside the family office. That person might handle the investment of long-only stocks, typically in passive funds.

For more information, see Chap. 7, "Evaluating Money Managers for Family Portfolios."

Step Seven

Review Your Investment Performance Regularly Most families will rely on you to produce periodic reports on the performance of the portfolio. Performance reporting systems are complex and expensive, but even so some larger families will find it useful to bring the performance reporting process in-house. That way the reports can be highly customized to the family's specifications.

Most families review their portfolios on a quarterly basis, but there is nothing magical about that timing. The main thing is to review performance regularly enough to spot trouble before it becomes serious, but not so often that you are tempted to make far too many changes based on short-term market events.

Performance reporting is partly science—the numbers need to be accurate and the reports need to be timely—and partly art. The "art" part means that the reports need to be user-friendly for the family. Most advisors will work with their clients to get the reports into a form that the family finds useful. See Chap. 14, in the section titled "Upgrading Portfolio Performance Systems."

Step Eight

Write an Investment Policy Statement Once the family has its governance structure and investment strategy in place, the next step is to *write it all down* in an investment policy statement or IPS.

A good IPS for a wealthy family will cover who the family is, how they govern themselves and make decisions (especially investment decisions), which individual portfolios are being managed, what the strategies are for each portfolio, how performance will be measured, and many other issues. You should draft the IPS but you must also work closely with the family to ensure it is a living, useful document. See Chap. 6, "Policy Statements for Wealthy Families."

Step Nine

Rethink Your Family Office As families build their businesses and as those businesses grow and become ever more profitable, most families will find it necessary or convenient to start a family office. At first, that office may be small and may rely on employees of the family business. The office might handle such mundane chores as accounting, bookkeeping, tax preparation, bill paying, and so on.

But once a large liquidity event is in sight, it may be time to reconsider the family office, its structure, and the activities it will undertake. For one thing, once the family's business has been sold, the senior family members may no longer have jobs. Or, rather, their job now is not to run the company but to run the liquid capital the company has produced.

Family members will need an office and will likely need different or additional resources. Decisions will have to be made about which activities to bring in-house and which to outsource. In short, a family office should continue to evolve as the family evolves, and a large liquidity event is a very important milestone for any family.

Step Ten

Relax If the family has successfully navigated all the foregoing steps and if they continue to monitor their portfolio regularly and make adjustments as necessary, the returns will take care of themselves. If your client is lying awake at night worrying about their money, you may have skipped one or more of the steps listed above.

11

What Is the Wealth For?

Let's assume that a family has been running a successful business for three generations. That business has now been sold, the closing has occurred, and the proceeds of $500 million have landed in the family's bank account. Now what?

That question can't be answered successfully without addressing a far more important question: *What is all this wealth for?*

While the family still owned the company it was clear what the company was for: to produce its products or services, to make a profit, to provide a livelihood to the company's employees, and to plough money back into the company's communities via taxes and, possibly, charitable contributions, sponsorships, or other financial support.

The family members could all relate to the company and its products or services. They were proud to be members of the family that owned that company.

But what is the *liquid* wealth for? How can anyone relate to something as ephemeral as wealth? What is going to hold the family together in the future?

And, for that matter, consider how the broader society is looking at this situation. When the family owned a company the family was viewed as a productive part of society. But now that company is owned by someone else and all the family owns is liquid wealth. Should society care about that family anymore? Is the family as a unit still a productive member of its broader society or has it, in effect, "retired"? Why not simply tax all of that wealth away?

Obviously, these are huge questions, but they are also real political issues: as this chapter was being written, some presidential candidates were advocating a tax on wealth.

© The Author(s) 2020
G. Curtis, *Advising the Ultra-Wealthy*, https://doi.org/10.1007/978-3-030-57605-9_11

Political issues are beyond the purview of this book, but what is *not* beyond the purview is the big question before the family: What is our wealth for? Obviously, every family will answer this question differently depending on their family history, the legacy they wish to leave behind them, and the values the family holds dear. But if you hope to advise ultra-wealthy families, you will have to help ensure that the family asks that question and answers it to its own satisfaction.

How to go about this process? First, make sure the family is asking the question. Too many families immediately start investing the proceeds of the sale of their business without any realistic idea of what the money is really *for*. Too many families promptly start fighting over the money. I have known families that started with over $1 billion of proceeds and blew through it *in a decade*. How? Over-spending. Internecine fighting. Extremely poor investment decision-making. But their real failure was not pausing to ask what their new-found wealth was for.

Here are some questions the family might start with: What does the family care about? What values does it hold above all others? When society looks back at the family 100 years from now, what legacy does the family want to have left?

Often, families will proceed as follows.

Does the Family Have a Competitive Advantage?

Suppose a family has just sold an operating business. While they still owned the business a family member served as CEO and several other family members served in various positions in the company. In addition, the family had hired several top executives and therefore had assembled a crack team of operating people.

Once the sale has been consummated, the buyer is unlikely to want or need all these people. Rather than allowing the experienced executive team to scatter to the winds, the family might say to itself, "We have a huge competitive advantage over most families because we have a team of people who know how to operate a consumer products business [for example]. Let's buy another business and grow it and sell it somewhere down the road."

The family could do this several times. And note that wealth will likely grow far faster in an operating company than it would have grown in a traditionally managed investment portfolio.

Of course, if the family is wise, it will set aside a significant portion of the sales proceeds as a "stay-rich portfolio," investing only the excess in buying a new company.

Does the Family Have Important Shared Values?

Most families that have recently become wealthy will have certain values they share. The values may be religious in nature; they may have to do with the need to "give back" to the society that allowed them to become wealthy. The values may relate to the desire to keep the family together (but see the next section below). The values may relate to the legacy the family wishes to leave behind it.

If the shared values are crucial to the family's identity, the family may adopt a "values statement," putting in writing what they believe and how they plan to live up to those values and to pass them on to future generations.

If a family wishes to stay together, it will be very important for older generations to share family stories, photos, and so on, with younger generations so that the latter will feel connected with the family members who have gone before them.

Does the Family Want to Stay Together or Go Their Separate Ways?

Most families will want to stay together and will work hard to keep the family connection strong. For example, they may plan annual family meetings and may establish a governance structure that will allow many family members to participate in the family's activities (see the last chapter).

But some families will not wish to stay together. They may wish to divide up the wealth and go their separate ways. In particular, as time goes by some family units may become dissatisfied with the way the family is managing itself and will want to take their share of the wealth and leave.

If you are hired by a family and that family stays together, you will continue to manage all the wealth. But if family members drift apart, you will likely lose the management of those assets unless you have stayed close to *all* the family members.

Investing in the Family's Human Capital

If a family manages its financial capital well, but its human capital poorly, the family will soon be broke. If a family manages its human capital well but its financial capital poorly, it may no longer be wealthy but it will be happy and productive. Your job, of course, is to ensure that the financial capital is well-managed. But you will also want to work with the family to keep its human capital intact.

There are many ways to nurture a family's human capital, but one important way is to encourage young family members to work hard even if they don't have a financial reason to work. A very good indication of a family that is losing its human capital is the percentage of family members who don't work.

Family members should be encouraged to pursue higher education, as appropriate, building their intellectual capital. They should be encouraged to become involved in the family governance, the family foundation, and so on.

Encourage the family to tell family stories and to preserve the best of them. This will include how the wealth was produced, from the first steps taken by the earliest family member to be involved in the business down through the generations. Talk about the struggles as well as the successes. Include stories about what the G1 family members were like, what G2 was like, and so on. Help younger family members feel like they are a part of something much bigger than themselves.

Many families work together to adopt values, statements, missions statements, and/or vision statements. There are many resources available to help you and your client through these processes,[1] as well as numerous consultants who are experienced at working with families on human capital issues.

A values statement, as its name implies, describes the values the family holds dear. A values statement is simply a list of the central values the family holds in highest esteem. A vision statement describes the family's objectives as a family: for example, should they stay together or go their separate ways? Should they invest together or separately? Should the family's philanthropic efforts be pooled or individualized? A vision statement is forward-looking: ideally, what would we like the family to look like decades or even centuries from now?

Sometimes, these statements can be special and deeply moving. A family might describe an abiding faith in God as their highest value and belief. A

---

[1] See, e.g., Kirby Rosplock, *The Complete Family Office Handbook: A Guide for Affluent Families and the Advisors Who Serve Them*, Bloomberg Press, 2014, especially Chap. 4.

family might be committed to service to others and to describe the obligations of service in fine detail.

But, frankly, most of these statements, when you go back and read them, seem generic and anodyne. Families who believe in "honesty and trustworthiness," who are "caring" and have a "strong moral code," probably didn't have to spend hours with a facilitator to come up with those ideas. Nonetheless, it is the *process* that is important, the very fact of the family working and talking together that matters. If the statement they came up with is merely soothing—not to say soporific—so what? The process itself was what mattered.

12

Socially Responsible Investing

Investing for reasons other than pure risk-adjusted returns has grown very rapidly in recent years. That activity goes by many names: socially responsible investing (SRI), ESG (Environmental, Social and Governance) investing, impact investing, ethical investing, mission-related investing, and so on.

Today, roughly 80% of the world's largest companies adhere to sustainable investing standards published by the Global Reporting Initiative (known as the "GRI Standards") and at least $20 trillion is currently invested in a socially responsible manner.

It's true that the vast majority of the capital engaged in socially responsible investing is institutional in nature: sovereign wealth funds, large pension plans and endowments, universities, and private foundations. But families have gotten into the act, too, and sometimes in a very big way.

Responsible investing is especially popular among younger family members—often referred to as "Next Gen." Millennials, for example, overwhelmingly see investing as a way to carry out their social agendas (67%), compared to 36% for Baby Boomers.

Very often, though, Next Gen family members who want to adopt socially responsible investing approaches find themselves wholly or partly thwarted by other more skeptical family members, by trustees and others with fiduciary responsibility, and even by the sheer complexity of the responsible investing field.

If you plan to enter the business of advising ultra-wealthy families today, you can't expect to succeed unless you develop a broad and deep understanding of socially responsible investing and of the main players in that field.

© The Author(s) 2020
G. Curtis, *Advising the Ultra-Wealthy*, https://doi.org/10.1007/978-3-030-57605-9_12

A full primer on SRI is far beyond the scope of this chapter, but here are some principles you may wish to keep in mind.

SRI Is Here to Stay

Whether or not you agree with the idea of investing for reasons other than pure risk-adjusted return, many wealthy families believe in it and younger generations of those families are often passionate about it. And they are backed up in their resolve by the trillions of dollars institutional investors are pouring into SRI.

Even investment funds that aren't specifically managed according to social principles nonetheless incorporate ESG factors into their investing, believing that at least some of these factors are in fact material to a stock's future performance. These investors are backed up by academic research, including that of George Serafeim at Harvard Business School.[1] The appropriateness of SRI in a fiduciary context remains problematic, but the law is moving very fast toward accepting at least some SRI investing by trustees and other fiduciaries.[2]

In other words, the days when advisors could simply ignore SRI and insist that their clients invest strictly for risk-adjusted return are long behind us, and those days aren't coming back.

How Families Invest in SRI

SRI investing is a vast and expanding field, but here are a few ways that families approach SRI.

Negative Screens Many investors simply don't want to own certain kinds of stocks—tobacco companies, gambling companies, coal mining companies, and so on. They will therefore wish to have their money invested in a portfolio that has been negatively screened to exclude such companies. Even fiduciaries like bank trustees will generally go along with this practice so long as the resulting tracking error of the portfolio remains within a reasonable range.

---

[1] See, e.g., Mozaffar Khan, George Serafeim and Aaron Yoon, "Corporate Sustainability: First Evidence on Materiality," *Accounting Review* 91, no. 6 (November 2016).
[2] See Max Schanzenbach and Robert Sitkoff, "Reconciling Fiduciary Duty and Social Conscience: The Law and Economics of ESG Investing by a Trustee," *Stanford Law Review*, Vol. 72 (2020).

ESG-Oriented Funds Many managers offer portfolios designed to focus on companies that are environmentally friendly, that have positive attitudes toward social issues (inclusiveness, community-awareness), and that follow best governance practices. Families are increasingly drawn to such funds, and fiduciaries will tend to accept them if the funds have competitive track records.

Impact Investing Impact investing is designed to achieve a "double bottom line," that is, to make a competitive return but also have a positive impact on the world in one way or another. Most impact investments tend to be private equity in nature, but not always. Families, especially younger generations, will often be much more focused on the "positive impact" than they are on the "competitive return," but fiduciaries may well balk.

Getting Good Advice

There are many, many organizations involved in SRI, and the popularity of the field means that a large chunk of these organizations are simply piling in hoping to make a quick buck. That said, there are also many very fine organizations that have long experience with SRI and to whom you can turn for advice and counsel. If the family you are working with wants to make a major foray into SRI, you may find it worthwhile to introduce the family to an SRI consultant or to a firm that, while it manages SRI money, is willing to sit down with your client and help educate them about best practices.

Pitfalls in SRI Investing

Partly because the field is still relatively new, there are many pitfalls that SRI investors will want to avoid, and you can provide a valuable service to your clients by keeping your eyes open for these issues.

Greenwashing Because socially responsible investing has become so popular, the financial industry has jumped into the sector with both feet. Some of the products are good, but many are simply ordinary investment products that have had a "green" label slapped on them. If your clients truly believe in the social issue they are pursuing, they will need to look carefully under the hood and make sure the fund they are looking at actually walks-the-walk.

Beware of the Financial Industry in General Sell-side financial firms are notorious for taking advantage of gullible investors, and socially responsible investors are no exception. If a story about the advantages of an impact fund seems too good to be true, it probably is. As an example, the Abraaj healthcare fund was launched to acquire and build hospitals in undeveloped nations, simultaneously bringing health care to remote regions and building valuable assets. Exactly why it was that Abraaj would succeed where others had failed was never clear, and in 2018, it all collapsed. The top three executives, including the director of impact investing, have been arrested and charged with fraud, and the fund itself is being dissolved.

Good Intentions Don't Count There are lots of areas of human endeavor where good intentions matter a lot, but socially responsible investing isn't one of them. In this area, good intentions, if not married to serious diligence, can make the world not a better place, but a much worse place. Consider the example of the switch to biofuels, which was hyped as a means of removing vast amounts of carbon from the air. Instead, huge swaths of forests were cut down to feed the biofuels appetite, releasing so much carbon into the atmosphere that scientists concluded it would take a century for the benefits of ethanol to overcome the initial carbon explosion and finally begin to reduce carbon emissions.

13

Trusts and Estate Planning

Some financial advisors offer estate planning as one of their main services, but most don't. Even if you don't, however, it's vitally important that you understand the main estate planning vehicles that ultra-wealthy families use and, especially, the *investment implications* of those vehicles.

Here is a brief survey of entities you are likely to encounter if you advise the ultra-wealthy, together with some of the investment implications.

Gifts, Charity, and Taxes

Wealthy clients are often confused and even paralyzed by the sheer number of decisions they are asked to make regarding investment strategies, financial planning advice, and tax issues. Nevertheless, when investment advisors peel back the jargon and focus clients on fundamental attitudes about wealth, the investment decision-making process becomes more straightforward.

Stated simply, investors can do only so many things with their wealth. First and foremost, clients can spend it. In this presentation, spending does not mean buying a yacht or a home or jewelry; such spending is simply reinvesting in nonfinancial assets, which is an asset allocation decision. True spending means *consumption (including taxes and gifts)*.

For most wealthy individuals, their investment portfolios are likely to be larger than the amount that can be consumed. Such clients possess only remaining options for their money: they can reinvest it, give it to their children, donate it to charity, or pay it in taxes.

© The Author(s) 2020
G. Curtis, *Advising the Ultra-Wealthy*, https://doi.org/10.1007/978-3-030-57605-9_13

Individuals have differing objectives. Some want to pass as much wealth as they can to their children, and others worry about spoiling them. Some are charitable; others are not. Many clients have not yet decided what they want to achieve with their wealth, so they feel uncertain about irrevocably committing to a plan of personal spending versus wealth transfer versus charitable giving. The only characteristic shared by nearly every client is that no one wants to pay more taxes than absolutely necessary.

Given the near universal aversion to the payment of taxes, the financial and legal communities have developed a series of clever techniques designed to minimize such payments. Two commonly employed methods are the charitable remainder unit trust (CRUT) and the grantor retained annuity trust (GRAT).

Charitable Remainder Unitrust A CRUT enables individuals to transfer assets to an irrevocable trust that is structured both to make an annual cash flow distribution back to them during their lifetime (fixed as a percentage of the trust's value) and to transfer the remaining assets to charity upon their death.

A client who establishes a CRUT benefits in a number of ways. First, the transfer of assets defers (or eliminates) the capital gains taxes associated with the sale of the low-cost assets. Second, the transfer creates a charitable tax deduction, which can provide a tax shelter for income or capital gains in the main portfolio. Third, the transfer generates an annual cash flow distribution back to the main portfolio. This cash flow establishes annual liquidity, and clients psychologically view the distributions from the CRUT as income. (Of course, clients can sell low-cost assets in their main portfolio and create liquidity for themselves, but most are reluctant to do so.) Finally, at the termination of the CRUT, the residual wealth transfers to charity, which satisfies the client's charitable intent.

Individuals interested purely in charity would not engage in a CRUT transaction but would instead make direct and current charitable gifts. The purpose of a CRUT, however, is to retain some benefit from the value of the assets gifted. Ultimately, either at the end of the CRUT's term or at the end of the grantor's life, the assets remaining in the CRUT pass to charity.

Investment implications: CRUTs are used when there is a serious charitable motive. Remember that taxes paid by the beneficiary are determined by the nature of the income at the trust level. Highest taxable income must be distributed first.

Grantor Retained Annuity Trust In broad terms, a GRAT has the same general objective as a CRUT: to transfer assets from an individual's portfolio to a trust in a way that minimizes or eliminates taxes.

As with a CRUT, the grantor (the individual funding the GRAT) derives a direct economic benefit from the arrangement because the GRAT pays an annuity back to his or her main portfolio. At the end of the GRAT's term, assets remaining in the trust after satisfying the required annual annuity payments are transferred to the next generation free of gift and estate tax.

Investment implications: Invest as aggressively as is consistent with the need to make the annuity payments (or more aggressively in the case of cascading GRATs). But the ultimate beneficiary isn't charity in this case, it's the next generation of the family.

Asset Protection Trusts These mainly offshore vehicles are often used by clients in litigious professions or who otherwise fear large legal judgments. They are similar to spendthrift trusts except that the trust is established in a foreign jurisdiction with laws that make it difficult for creditors to enforce their rights (often via very short statutes of limitation). A key provision is the presence of a "protector" who will not be subject to US court orders. Unlike spendthrift trusts, with an APT the presence of the donor as a discretionary beneficiary does not render the gift to the trust incomplete; hence, APTs can effectively be used to remove assets from the estate of the donor.

APTs must be created before a judgment is entered against the donor and preferably before any claim has been asserted. *Investment implications*: All US taxes must be paid on income and gains as they occur, exactly as though the trust were a domestic trust. Consequently, the investment considerations will be similar to those posed by a domestic portfolio. Assets placed in APTs may remain in trust longer, and hence have a longer investment time horizon associated with them, than the same assets may have had when held directly and domestically.

Investment implications: These depend on the beneficiary's objectives.

Dynasty Trusts A dynasty trust is a term typically applied to any trust that is designed to last for several generations. Dynasty trusts created in states that have abolished the rule against perpetuities can theoretically last forever. *Investment implications*: These vehicles have very long investment time horizons and few income demands. Invest aggressively, consistent with fiduciary principles.

Generation Skipping Trusts Gifts that skip a generation are subject to very high taxes. However, parents can create a trust and allocate their GST exemptions to it (being careful to avoid gift taxes). GST trusts are limited in most states by the rule against perpetuities, but by creating the trust in a jurisdiction that has repealed the rule the trust can last theoretically forever. A GST dynasty trust can be leveraged considerably by combining it with a CLUT. *Investment implications*: These vehicles have very long investment time horizons and few income demands. Invest aggressively, consistent with fiduciary principles.

Insurance Wraps These are not technically trusts. Placing a tax-inefficient asset inside an insurance product (usually a modified endowment contract or a variable annuity contract) causes the tax consequences to pass to the insurance company while the gains remain in the policy as increasing cash value. The insured can access the cash value through low-cost policy loans or simple cash withdrawals. Many insurance wraps are structured through offshore insurance companies to avoid strict state rules on investment options. The ongoing cost of these programs is an important issue. *Investment implications*: These vehicles are useful to shelter the income from growth assets that generate substantial ordinary income or short-term capital gains, for example, non-directional hedge funds. Keep in mind that the insured cannot select the investments inside the policy.

Intentionally Defective Trusts An intentionally defective trust is one which will not be includable in the grantor's estate but on which the grantor pays all taxes incurred on the trust assets even though the income or appreciation is going to the children. These taxes represent an additional untaxed gift. A trust can be "defective" by giving the grantor the right to "sprinkle" income or principal among a group of beneficiaries, by retaining the power to reacquire the trust assets by substituting property of equal value, or if the trust income can be distributed to the grantor's spouse. *Investment implications*: Since the donor pays all taxes, his or her tax picture must be kept in mind. It is usually preferable to invest in assets that generate long-term capital gains.

Private Foundations Foundations can be established as trusts or corporations. Corporations are much simpler to administer, and they avoid bizarre state limits on investments. Trusts, however, are better equipped to preserve family control over the generations. A private foundation is a grantmaking organization which must make grants equal to 5% or more of its assets each year; pays a 1% or 2% excise tax, depending on the scale of the grantmaking; must file a Form 990-PF with the IRS every year; and must make available to the public either its 990-PF or an annual report. Note that most foundations will likely find themselves the target of unsolicited funding proposals, and failure to respond to these funding requests can harm the family's reputation. Gifts to private foundations are limited to 20% of Adjusted Gross Income.

Investment implications: Many foundations invest far too conservatively. During extended bear markets (as in the 1970s), the 5% payout requirement, plus the excise tax, can actually amount to a much higher percentage of the current asset base.

14

Strengthening Your Existing Knowledge

In this chapter I discuss several issues that are already familiar to financial advisors who work with families of any size. Hence, I only touch on aspects of the issues that are peculiar to ultra-wealthy families, ways in which you will likely need to modify what you are already doing now. I also touch on an important issue— involving next generation family members and family transitions—that financial advisors may be only tangentially involved in, but which is crucial to maintaining the relationship with the family following a generational transition.

Asset Allocation for Ultra-Wealthy Families

As all financial advisors know, asset allocation is the critical building block for any family portfolio, and advisors are adept at creating asset allocation strategies for their clients. To be competitive in the ultra-high net worth sector, however, advisors will need to address a number of issues that are more or less specific to the ultra-wealthy sector.

I am assuming in this book that my readers are already familiar with the concept of asset allocation and the techniques associated with that process. The following bullet points address how that existing skill set will need to be upgraded when working with ultra-wealthy families:

- Asset allocation strategies must be designed from the bottom up; that is, they must be highly customized for each family. Simply offering predesigned

© The Author(s) 2020
G. Curtis, *Advising the Ultra-Wealthy*, https://doi.org/10.1007/978-3-030-57605-9_14

Moderate, Aggressive, and Conservative strategies won't work with ultra-wealthy families.

- Virtually all ultra-wealthy families will have not one portfolio that needs to be designed, but many. You will need to design appropriate portfolios for G1, G2, and G3. There will be specific portfolios for individual family units, individual trusts, IRA accounts, and family foundations. Some ultra-wealthy families will have literally hundreds of family trusts. Once this has been done, you will need to roll up the individual portfolios to make sure that, at the aggregate family level, the money is invested sensibly.

- Often, it will be necessary to form investment partnerships or LLCs so that smaller family units can invest in hedge and private equity funds and be able to control their own specific exposures. The accounting and book-keeping for these vehicles is complex and will need to be handled either by a sophisticated custody bank or by engaging an accounting firm.

- You will need to design portfolios using *after-tax* inputs. Ultra-wealthy families pay high taxes and their portfolios need to be efficient on an after-tax basis. Thus, you will need to convert pre-tax returns, risks, and correlations into after-tax inputs based on the family's specific tax regime. A family that pays federal, New York State, and New York City taxes will be in a very different position from a family that lives in a state with no income or capital gains tax and no municipal tax. Families will want to understand how you have taken taxes into account in designing their portfolios.

- Speaking of inputs, you will need to be prepared to justify to your family clients the inputs you are using. If your expected returns for asset classes going forward are nothing more than the actual returns for those asset classes over the past 10 years, your clients aren't likely to be impressed.

- In addition to using traditional mean variance optimization (MVO) techniques, you will likely find it useful to supplement this approach by incorporating Black-Litterman analyses into your final design product. If you are unfamiliar with Black-Litterman you will need to bone up on it.

- You will want to take into account the problem of "fat tails": the fact that capital markets outcomes aren't in fact shaped exactly like a bell curve. Instead, extreme outcomes (both good and bad) occur far more frequently than MVO would suggest. Thus, a considerable amount of judgment needs to be applied to the final asset allocation recommendation you present to the client.

- In designing portfolios for ultra-wealthy families, it is crucial to keep in mind that this capital is irreplaceable. Becoming ultra-wealthy is a one-in-a-million outcome—it's not likely to happen again to the same family.

Reaching for return might endear you to the client in the short term, but it can come back to haunt you when markets turn south.

- In addition to long-term strategic asset allocation, you will need to have a process in place to deal with *tactical* asset allocation. Tactical changes can easily slip over into market timing, so you will want to put into place strict guidelines to avoid simply overreacting to transient market events. Since tactical moves in a portfolio usually result in taxes, you will want to add that factor to your decision-making process. Speaking very broadly, you will likely find it more effective to move a client's portfolio away from sectors that appear to be overvalued, rather than moving portfolios toward areas that appear to be undervalued. Avoiding large losses is usually more appreciated by clients than a bit of incremental return.

- Many "smaller" clients will be invested in fewer asset classes and sectors than ultra-wealthy families will wish to do. Thus, if you don't currently use long/short hedge, non-directional hedge, venture capital, buyouts, or mezzanine, you will need to become familiar with these sectors and how best to model them. The same is true of geographical exposure. Most "smaller" families won't be invested in Asian private equity, but most ultra-wealthy investors will be.

Recurring Mistakes Ultra-Wealthy Families Make

Every experienced financial advisor knows all too well that family investors tend to make recurring mistakes in managing their investments. Indeed, one could make the argument that the single most important duty of a financial advisor is to prevent clients from making these mistakes.

In this chapter I will focus on two issues. First, I will outline some of the common mistakes investors make, but with the emphasis on how such mistakes play out in the portfolios of wealthy families. Second, I will identify a few mistakes that are characteristically made mainly by wealthy families.

Buying High and Selling Low

Because investing is an emotional, as well as a rational, activity, families seem to be hard-wired to do the wrong thing at the wrong time. When markets are going up, investors are too optimistic and tend to overpay for investment assets. When markets are going down, investors are too pessimistic and tend to sell when they should hold—or even buy.

While this phenomenon affects almost all investors, it can be especially problematic for wealthy families. Most wealthy families are, or should be, capital preservation-oriented. After all, they are already wealthy, and therefore, the benefit of getting even richer is, for most families, far outweighed by the possibility of losing their wealth.

Overpaying for stocks during strong market environments significantly increases the risk level of a portfolio, migrating a wealthy family away from a sensible capital-preservation strategy to a much higher-risk strategy. Suppose, for example, that a family begins with a portfolio that is 65% invested in equities. If that family keeps buying expensive stocks out of over-enthusiasm, its equity exposure could easily rise to 70% or 75%.

Then, when the market corrects, the family will lose millions of dollars. That unexpected loss will then cause the family's tolerance for risk to atrophy. Instead of buying stocks at the new, more attractive prices, the family will likely remain out of the market and will not benefit from the subsequent recovery. If this happens several times, the family will soon find that it is no longer wealthy.

Obviously, advisors who wish to work with the ultra-wealthy need to develop strategies designed to avoid this sort of behavior. Here are a couple of options:

- Help the family recruit an "investment committee" that can counsel the family when it seems to be going off the rails. Family investment committees tend to be less formal than institutional committees. They also tend to consist less of financial professionals and more of trusted advisors from other professions. What a family needs to have around the table is people whose judgment the family feels it can rely on. Those people might be attorneys, tax accountants, bankers, trustees, or simply friends.
- Try to get younger family members into the conversation. Older people tend to get very nervous following big losses in the markets because their time horizons are shorter. When they panic and sell out, they often have a hard time reinvesting. Younger people, with much longer time horizons, can often play a constructive role.
- During a calm period in the markets, recommend that the family adopt, as part of its investment policy statement, a description of how it will behave during market crises. (An example appears in the Exhibit to this chapter.)

Being Pennywise and Pound-Foolish

Many middle-income investors engage financial advisors while having only the dimmest idea of what their total fees and costs will be. But wealthy families tend to focus obsessively on those topics when interviewing potential advisors. This is in part because of the large absolute dollar amount of the fee—a family with several hundred million dollars to invest can easily pay several hundred thousand dollars a year in financial advisory fees.

Another explanation for the over-focus on fees is that wealthy families are often taken advantage of. The price of almost everything seems to go up as soon as the seller learns that the buyer has deep pockets. Thus, the emphasis on fees represents a natural defense against being over-charged.

I have watched fee-conscious families end up with very weak advisors—indeed, in some cases unscrupulous advisors—simply because those advisors were the low bidders.

There isn't a great deal that can be done in these cases, because you don't yet have a relationship with the family. But here are a few ideas:

- Since fee competition will be an ongoing challenge, you should prepare in advance a justification for your fees. This justification can't be entirely qualitative because the low bidder will match you word for word. It needs to be quantitative and straightforward: your fees are justified based on the improved performance you will bring to the account. After all, if your fee is $25,000 higher than someone else's, that difference can easily be made up by even modest outperformance. Consider a $100 million portfolio—at the smaller end of the ultra-wealthy spectrum. If your (weak) competitor can produce an annualized return of 7%, while you can produce an annualized return of merely 7.1%, your performance will bring the client four times your fee in the first year. The point of this exercise is to put the $25,000 fee difference in perspective.
- Try to open a dialogue with whoever the family's most trusted nonfinancial advisor is. That person is less likely to be paranoid about being over-charged—indeed, he or she will have very often been in your seat, having to compete against bottom-feeding competitors.

Trouble Making Decisions; Not Taking Advice

When only one or two family members are making investment decisions (usually the patriarch and matriarch), things tend to work fairly smoothly.

But as the next generation reaches adulthood and wants to be involved, decision-making can slow down. The solution obviously isn't to keep younger family members on the outside looking in—it's crucially important, in fact, to involve younger family members.

The solution has be the creation of a governance structure in the family that allows a broader group of family members to participate, but which doesn't slow down or otherwise corrupt decision-making. A governance structure can be quite simple. For example, an investment committee could consist of the patriarch and matriarch plus the three oldest adult children. Assuming that the patriarch and matriarch will tend to agree on issues, they will prevail unless all the adult children vote in opposition.

More complex governance structures often grow as the family expands. For example, there might be a family board elected by all adult family members. That board might appoint an investment committee consisting of both family members and trusted outsiders. Sometimes the decisions of the investment committee are binding; sometimes they are advisory. The roles of the board and committee need to be specified in writing, of course. (An example of an investment committee charter for a family is available in Chap. 6.)

A somewhat similar mistake occurs when a family doesn't accept its advisor's recommendations. Sometimes this is because the family doesn't feel comfortable managing liquid assets and they simply can't "pull the trigger." Other times the problem is that the family's trust in its advisor isn't very high. After a few years of this the family realizes that its investment performance isn't very good, and instead of blaming itself, it blames the advisor.

In my experience, this issue is one of the most difficult to fix. Sometimes it's possible to get through to a trusted family advisor—a lawyer, for example—who can convince the family of the importance of taking expert advice. But of course this is a high-risk gambit. The family may simply decide that the reason they're not taking your advice is because they don't trust you and they will terminate their relationship with you.

One interesting initiative that can sometimes help is to convince the family to establish a small "side" portfolio that will follow all the advisor's recommendations. For example, if the family has $500 million, the side portfolio might be $50 million. If, over time, that portfolio performs well, it might go a long way to boosting the family's comfort level with the advisor's recommendations.

Fear of the Unknown

Wealthy families didn't become wealthy because they were stupid or exercised bad judgment. On the other hand, it's a rare family that became wealthy through investing in marketable securities. (Warren Buffett is a major exception, of course.)

When a family owns a business its entire net worth is bound up in that business with no diversification at all. Yet families are quite comfortable with that situation. They know their businesses inside and out; they know their customers, their suppliers, and their competitors.

But once the business has been sold and the family is managing a large pool of liquid capital, all this changes. They are now trying to navigate a world they don't understand very well, certainly not as well as they understood the family company.

Very often this situation results in an unwillingness to invest in funds or sectors that are not straightforward. Stocks and bonds are easily understood, and families intuitively understand private equity investing. But hedge funds and quantitative strategies that involve artificial intelligence and/or machine learning are something else altogether. Yet, without these more complicated strategies, the portfolio will be considerably less robust.

A family investment committee can often be helpful in these situations, at least if it contains a few experienced investors. Beyond that it is mainly going to be a process of educating the family about how complex strategies work and why they are important.

For example, if the family declines to accept your recommendation of a complex fund, you can continue to discuss it with the family at future meetings, showing how the fund has performed and how the portfolio would have been better off if the family had invested in the fund. The point is not to say "I told you so," but simply to allow the family to gradually become more comfortable with the fund as they observe how it performs.

Disagreements About Socially Responsible Investing

Socially responsible investing (SRI) is discussed earlier in this book (see Chap. 12). For now, however, I want to focus on intra-family disagreements about SRI.

SRI has grown enormously in recent years, but it is still mainly an approach that is favored by institutional investors and younger investors. As a result, you will frequently encounter a very common situation: young-but-adult children passionately want the family to follow socially responsible principles while the older generation remains skeptical.

You could spend a great deal of time and burn up a great deal of hard-earned goodwill trying to bring the family to an agreement about SRI. But, frankly, why bother? There are specialists in the SRI field who deal with this issue all the time and who are far more likely to bring the family together over SRI than you are.

If the family isn't willing to engage a specialist and you find yourself stuck with the job, here are some suggestions:

- The core of the disagreements over SRI revolves around these issues: Will an SRI portfolio underperform a more traditional portfolio? If so, is the degree of underperformance tolerable, given the better alignment with the family's values? These disagreements simply can't be resolved factually because for every analysis showing SRI performs as well or better than traditional portfolios, there are analyses that show the opposite. Perhaps some day the evidence will tilt decidedly one way or the other, but until then the family will simply agree-to-disagree.
- Given the above, sometimes the best way to move forward is to do both SRI and traditional investing. For example, large family trusts that benefit many different individuals and generations could remain invested traditionally. On the other hand, smaller trusts benefitting one individual plus his or her descendants could be invested in a socially responsible manner. As time goes by and the results are in, either the family will expand SRI or it won't. After all, regardless of the broader outcomes of SRI investing, some individual families will be good at it and some won't.

Failing to Learn

As noted above, most families became wealthy without ever learning much about managing very large sums of private capital—their high net worths were tied up in an illiquid company. But they had to learn to operate that company effectively. Indeed, most ultra-wealthy families built that wealth over several generations. Each new generation had to learn to run the company, often starting at the bottom and working their way up.

The same thing needs to happen with managing liquid capital. The family needs to learn how to do it and every new generation has to learn in its turn. One way to accomplish this, of course, is to learn by trial and error. That's probably how the founding generation of the family learned to operate its business. But that's also why most businesses fail. Learning to manage a portfolio by trial and error will likely fail too.

Instead, a family needs to learn under your tutelage, and it's a very important part of your job to make sure that learning happens. Here are some things you can do to make sure that learning does in fact happen:

- Every meeting with the family, every conversation with the family, needs to be a learning experience. Speak plain English to them and explain everything, no matter how simple it seems to you. If you have the slightest doubt whether the family is getting what you're saying or recommending, *ask them*: "Sophie, did you understand what I meant when I said that small banks stocks aren't an asset class?"
- Make every meeting with the family educationally useful. Invite one of the family's managers to appear at or call into meetings periodically. Make sure the family members understand what the manager is saying—intervene if you have to and restate the point in plain English. Occasionally, devote a portion of a meeting to learning about some aspect of investing: What are hedge funds? How does private equity work? Why is portfolio volatility so important?
- When a new generation comes along and is old enough to begin to participate, hold specific educational sessions with them. If you're not a good teacher, bring in someone who is.

If you've worked with a family for five years and they don't know any more about investing than they did when you were engaged, you have failed that family.

Wanting to Invest Like Yale

The extraordinary success of the Yale endowment under the leadership of David Swensen is the envy of investors everywhere. It's hardly surprising, then, that many families want to emulate that experience, which typically means an investment portfolio designed according to the "endowment model." Generally speaking, this means much lower-than-usual exposures to traditional stocks, extremely low exposures to bonds, and much higher exposures to "alternative" assets like private equity, venture capital, real estate, oil and natural gas, and hedge funds.

Adopting an endowment model *is almost always a very bad idea for a family investor.* In fact, adopting an endowment model is usually a bad idea even for an endowment.

People, including David Swensen,[1] have written entire books about the endowment model and why it is inappropriate for most investors. For purposes of this chapter, I will merely make the following observations:

- Every investor needs to design a portfolio that is *right for that investor.* Yale's portfolio may be right for Yale and for a few other extraordinarily large and well-advised endowments, but it is wrong for most investors, especially families. Families need to start by examining who they are as a family, how much experience they have had with investing liquid capital, how they feel about investment risk, what their spending needs are, what their real investment time horizon is, what the size of their asset pool is, what sort of investment talent they can access, and similar factors. Then, building from the bottom up, a family can design a portfolio that addresses those needs and constraints. That portfolio is unlikely to look much like the Yale portfolio.
- Yale has David Swensen and families don't.
- Yale was among the first large investors to expand into alternative assets, especially venture capital and private equity. The portfolios Yale was able to build as the first mover cannot be duplicated by anyone else.
- Institutions like Yale can afford to take much more risk than families can take because they have advantages families don't have: they don't pay taxes; their huge size means lower fees and transaction costs; they can raise money from loyal alums.

Of course, this doesn't mean that families shouldn't invest in alternative assets. It does mean, however, that putting 70% of their assets into such investments is likely to prove extremely foolish.

Nextgen and Family Transitions

In a very real sense, ultra-wealthy families are in the business of managing capital. Like any business, the decision makers will eventually age out and will need to be replaced by younger people. In order for that transition to work

---

[1] See Swensen, *Pioneering Portfolio Management* (describing the Yale model) and *Unconventional Success* (advocating a very different approach for most investors).

smoothly it's important that younger family members be educated in the stewardship of the family's assets. As the family's financial advisor, you may or may not become involved in teaching younger family members about investing, but it is almost always the case that the financial advisor will be involved somehow in the process.

The Meaning of Stewardship

Stewardship includes education in the investment process, of course, but it goes far beyond that. Whatever obligations young members of ultra-wealthy families are expected to take on over the years, none will be well-handled unless those young people are raised to be productive human beings. The human capital of a family will always be more important than the financial capital. If the human capital degrades, the financial capital will simply go away: shirtsleeves-to-shirtsleeves in three generations. Thus, young people need to be taught the value of work, the importance of participating in family meetings and governance, the need to find meaning in life beyond wealth.

Maintaining the family's human capital should be Job #1 for most ultra-wealthy families. This includes:

- Intellectual capital. Are young people in the family getting educated, staying in school, continuing to learn and improve their ability to thrive in a rapidly changing and competitive world? Are they remaining curious about their world and their place in it?
- Social capital. How well do family members get along? Can they disagree without being disagreeable? Is attendance at family meetings strong? How well do family members get along with their neighbors and the broader community? Are marriages strong?
- Spiritual capital. Many families are deeply religious and their faith is an important part of what holds them together. But beyond religion, what is it that is important to the family that bonds it together? Spiritual capital understands that wealth doesn't define the family.

Learning to steward the family and its assets successfully doesn't happen overnight; it's a lifelong process. Whether or not you are directly involved in working with Nextgen family members, your ability to remain as the family's advisor following a generational transition will depend critically on how well the family's young people have been nurtured and taught.

Upgrading Portfolio Performance Systems

If your current performance management system works well only with mutual funds and similar commingled vehicles, you will need to invest in an upgrade. Ultra-wealthy families use mutual funds, index funds, and similar vehicles, but they mainly use separate accounts—managers who buy and sell individual securities specifically for the family's own account. Your new system will also have to deal with hedge funds, private equity funds, and similar kinds of investments that are commonly found in ultra-high net worth portfolios.

Ultra-wealthy families and their sophisticated investment committees will also want to see complex portfolio analytics that go beyond internal rate of return calculations. For example, you will likely want to be able to show your clients risk analyses of various sort, performance attribution, security-level reconciliation, secure client portals, and so on.

This technology isn't cheap, so for some firms this necessary upgrade could be a deal-killer.

The Family's Goals and Objectives

In a sense, working with ultra-wealthy families on setting goals and objectives can be simpler than dealing with smaller families on the same subject. For families in the mass affluent category, different and often competing objectives like buying a home, paying for college, and funding retirement can present complex issues. Indeed, an entire literature has grown up around the subject of multiple investor goals. (See the work of Jean L.P. Brunel, especially his book, *Goals-Based Wealth Management: An Integrated and Practical Approach to Changing the Structure of Wealth Advisory Practices* [Wiley Finance, 2015].)

But with enormously wealthy families, the traditional objectives and goals make little sense. These families don't need to save up for college or retirement (although they may need to ensure sufficient liquidity is available as needed). For wealthy families the key question is how they weigh the objective of *staying rich* against the objective of *getting richer*.

Overwhelmingly, wealthy families tend to be capital preservation-oriented; that is, they recognize how rare becoming wealthy is and their first priority is to stay wealthy. But there are a few families who are willing to accept the additional risk required to become even wealthier.

In general, these different approaches are easy to spot, but sometimes, families can surprise their advisors—and even themselves. This tends to happen when a family with little investment experience suddenly becomes very rich via a liquidity event.

Exhibit A

Managing the Smith Family Portfolios
During Periods of Market Dislocation
Adopted _____

The purpose of this Exhibit to the family's Investment Policy Statement is to set forth principles for managing the portfolios during periods of economic crisis and/or severe capital markets dislocation.

The Likelihood of Encountering Severe Markets

If investment returns were truly randomly distributed (along the familiar Bell Curve), then extreme market conditions would be quite rare and most investors would have little reason to worry about or prepare for them. In fact, however, investment outcomes are abnormally distributed; that is, they have "fat tails," meaning that extreme outcomes—especially extremely bad outcomes—are much more common than one might expect. Within the investment lifetimes of the current advisors to the family, for example, very extreme negative outcomes occurred in 1973–1974, 1987, 2000, 2001 (briefly), 2008, and 2020. Successfully managing portfolios through such crises is key to the preservation of the family's capital, since mistakes made during such periods can be catastrophic. For example, investors who panicked and converted their portfolios entirely to cash during the severe market conditions mentioned above—and then remained in cash—never recovered from the losses they incurred. The typical mistake is to ride the market most of the way down, then capitulate and switch to a much lower risk portfolio which cannot possibly appreciate enough to make up for the losses. In that sense, mistakes made during market crises can cause a "permanent" loss of capital.

Navigating Treacherous Market Environments

The process of navigating through treacherous market conditions consists of a series of steps beginning before the crisis happens and continuing well after the crisis has passed, as discussed below:

(a) Market crises don't happen out of the blue. They almost always begin with a long period of appreciating prices which eventually exceed reasonable valuation levels as measured by historic metrics. Thus, the first step in dealing with treacherous markets is not to "drink the Kool-Aid" in the first place. As prices rise well above historic norms, thoughtful investors will begin to take profits off the table, reinvesting in lower risk assets and maintaining their long-term asset allocation targets. It is important to remember that as equity prices increase and, therefore, equity allocations in the portfolio increase, the risk level of the portfolio increases far beyond the level originally established as appropriate for the family.

(b) As equity prices continue to rise, losing touch with any sense of economic reality, the portfolios should begin to sell enough stocks to move below target equity allocations and toward minimum equity allocations. With pricing at extreme levels, the danger is all on the downside, and therefore, even target equity allocations are dangerous to the health of the portfolio. It is important to keep in mind that losses are more harmful to capital than gains are helpful. To take an extreme, but hardly outlandish, example, if a $1 million portfolio rises 80%, it will be worth $1.8 million. If it then declines by 80%, the capital will be worth only $640,000. (This exact math occurred to investors in technology stocks in the late 1990s and early 2000s.) Of course, it is difficult to measure precisely when markets are approaching extreme levels of pricing. However, traditional metrics such as the price/earnings ratio, price-to-book ratio, and dividend yield are all useful indicators. During Bull Market environments these metrics should be closely monitored by the Investment Committee.

(c) Patience is required during stages (a) and (b) because markets will still be rising and other, less thoughtful, investors will be making better returns than investors who are following the strategies set forth above. As noted, however, the risk they are exposing their portfolios to is growing rapidly. Note, also, that it is typically unwise to allow equity allocations to fall below the minimum range, as this puts the family too far out of the market. During periods when markets appear to be extremely overvalued, the Investment Committee can further insulate the portfolio from decline by employing highly defensive managers.

(d) Eventually, equity markets will reprice (that is, they will decline in value), and investors who have continued to own (or, worse, buy) equities will get clobbered. In the broad panic, investors will sell stocks in large quantities and equity prices will often decline far below fair value as measured by historic norms. At this point, many (possibly most) investors will be in a state of shock and unable to think sensibly about market valuations. However, investors who were less exposed to equities (like the family) will be presented with an opportunity to buy back into the market at attractive prices.

(e) Typically, the repurchase of equities should begin at approximately the point when stock prices have fallen below long-term averages and the buying should continue as stock prices continue to decline (or rise) until the family has reached its target equity allocations. (This is the averaging-in process.) Assuming that economic conditions have improved to the point where traditional valuation metrics are appropriate, the family might even continue to purchase equities until they are above their target allocations, (though not above their maximum allocations), continuing to take advantage of attractive pricing.

(f) By the time the economic crisis is over and equity prices have resumed normal valuations, the family will—by following these steps—have out-performed the great majority of other investors, increasing the family's competitive advantage.

15

Miscellaneous Issues that Affect the Ultra-Wealthy

Asset Custody

Smaller family investors, using mutual funds, index funds, and ETFs, present few problems with custody and performance reporting. But once the numbers get large and separate accounts proliferate, asset custody becomes both critically important and highly complex.

A custodian—typically a very large bank—safeguards the family's investment assets by holding them in a segregated account owned by the investor. The fact that the account is segregated is important. Segregated assets are formally "segregated" from the assets of the bank that is serving as the custodian. In the unlikely event that the bank should go bankrupt, the investor's assets will not be subject to the claims of the bank's creditors.

This is not the case, it is important to note, with brokerage firms that are acting as a custodian. If the broker goes under, the investor's assets go under, too, and are available to the brokerage firm's creditors. This happened during the bankruptcy of Lehman Brothers and investors who thought their money was safe lost hundreds of millions of dollars.

A master custodian will typically provide all or most of the following services:

- Provide for safekeeping of the client's investment assets domestically and internationally
- Maintain accurate and timely records of the client's investments
- Consolidate assets as necessary for reporting purposes
- Clear and settle trades made at the direction of the client's money managers

© The Author(s) 2020
G. Curtis, *Advising the Ultra-Wealthy*, https://doi.org/10.1007/978-3-030-57605-9_15

- Transfer assets as directed only by the client
- Pay bills for various services (e.g., money manager fees)
- Provide multicurrency reporting for international assets
- Prepare reports on a cash or accrual basis
- Report transactions on a trade or settlement date basis
- Maintain records and process trades on a tax-lot basis
- Maintain tax characteristics (interest, dividends, cost basis, etc.)
- Maintain compliance monitoring systems to ensure that managers adhere to whatever investment guidelines the client has put in place
- Provide unitized accounting and interim valuations
- Prepare tax returns
- Maintain accounting for family investment partnerships (note that only a few very high-end custodians offer this service)
- Serve as the book of record for all financial transactions

Asset custody is, frankly, a lousy business. It is capital intensive and low margin, and most firms that offer custody do so as a loss-leader. These firms believe that if they control a family's assets via their custody platform, the family will be likely to hire them to provide other services—especially asset management.

In fact, most firms won't offer custody services unless they can also manage some of the money. You will therefore find it prudent to ascertain which managed products the firm offers that are either best-in-class or at least acceptable. The best place to look for such products will be in index funds and bonds.

Managing Investment Taxes

The tax issue has been mentioned many times in these pages but I bring it up here to emphasize that if you wish to be successful advising ultra-wealthy families you will need to take taxes into account at *every step* along the way. It's true, of course, that the tax tail shouldn't wag the investment dog, but it's also true that failure to structure your advice in tax-efficient ways will cost your clients a lot of money.

Briefly:

Asset Allocation Once you have estimated expected future returns for each asset class, you will need to convert those returns into after-tax numbers (based on the client's federal, state and local, tax situation) before you run a mean variance optimization. Otherwise, you will have created a strategy that might be suitable for a tax-exempt investor, but that is unsuitable for your client.

Manager Selection   Managers that are appropriate for endowments or pension plans may well be completely inappropriate for your highly taxed ultra-wealthy client. To be suitable for taxable families, a manager must produce enough alpha to overcome all its costs, *including taxes*. Some managers—venture capital and buyouts funds—will be naturally tax-efficient, producing mainly deferred long-term capital gains. Other managers, especially hedge funds, will be naturally tax-inefficient, producing mainly short-term gains that are taxed as ordinary income. One way to create tax "room" for such managers is to invest part of the client's money in tax-aware index funds that capture short-term losses as they naturally occur through market volatility. These short-term losses can then be offset against the short-term gains produced by the hedge funds.

Offsetting Gains and Losses   Every quarter you should look through your clients' portfolios and note large gains and losses. It may be prudent to ask managers holding large losses to realize those losses and then, 30 days later (to avoid the wash sale rule), buy them back. In the meantime, it is usually possible for the manager to buy other securities with similar characteristics in order to avoid being out of the market for a month. Also, try to use managers who will be cognizant of tax lots when selling.

After-Tax Performance Reporting   Theoretically, all investment performance should be calculated on an after-tax basis, since investors can't spend money that must be paid to the government. Your client's after-tax return is the difference between the client's starting market value and the ending market value plus any dividends, interest, or other income received and minus any costs or taxes paid. The practical realities of producing sensible after-tax results, however, are daunting, primarily because of the many assumptions that need to be made. For example, when will assets be sold and the tax incurred? Next week? Next year? At death?

Working with Family Offices

Many wealthy families will have established a family office. The office may be rudimentary—handling bookkeeping and accounting matters, perhaps helping with travel arrangements—or it may be a large, fully staffed office with its own in-house investment capabilities (a chief investment officer, perhaps a few analysts). In any event, you will find that your relationship with the family office is important to the success of the engagement.

Virtually all family offices are understaffed and struggle to respond to their family's needs, and you will likely find that the office staff will frequently turn to you to help them out. This will be something you have to manage. If you drop everything whenever the office calls, the profitability of the relationship will suffer hugely. If you fail to help the family office, you will lose the relationship.

The main thing to remember is that you will want to think of the family office as your *partner*, not as your enemy. The more you can help make the family office staff look good to the family, the better your overall relationship will be. Remember that the office staff interact with family members vastly more than you do.

It can help to discuss these kinds of issues thoroughly with the family office staff before you execute an advisory agreement (see below). The agreement could describe the allocation of responsibilities between you and the office. It could anticipate that the office may from time to time need or wish to rely more heavily on you, and the agreement could contemplate an additional fee for such services. (That fee will itself serve as an encouragement to the office not to over-rely on you.)

Family office workers are overwhelmingly dedicated professionals deeply committed to the welfare of the families they work for. As noted, they are often under-resourced. The more smoothly you can handle your interface with these professionals, the happier you will be, the happier they will be, and the happier the ultimate client will be.

Your Advisory Agreement

The Securities and Exchange Commission's rules require that advisors have agreements with their clients, but those rules don't specifically address the content of the agreements. You undoubtedly have a form of agreement that you normally use, but as you begin to work with the ultra-wealthy, you will likely find it useful—or necessary—to alter the standard agreement.

Some wealthy families will ask their high-powered attorneys to go over your agreement with a fine-tooth comb. These attorneys might be simply trying to justify their (exorbitant) fees, but more likely, they are doing their best to protect their client. It is also likely to be the case that the attorneys are used to seeing far more robust and complex agreements than the standard form you are using, and they will want to beef it up. Finally, the affairs of ultra-wealthy families are highly complex, and your advisory agreement with them should acknowledge that complexity.

On the other hand, ideally you want your agreement to be written in "plain English." Interestingly, the Securities and Exchange Commission's *A Plain English Handbook* (available at https://www.sec.gov/pdf/handbook.pdf) boasts an introduction by Warren Buffett, who remarks that when you use plain English, "you will be amazed at how much smarter your readers will think you have become."

A family member who is not a professional investor or a lawyer should be able to read your agreement and understand it. Family office staff shouldn't have to consult attorneys to figure out what your agreement says. Thus, you should feel free to push back against lawyers who are advocating overly complex terms or arcane jargon and insist that the language be more clear. On the other hand, you should also expect that the simpler agreement you have been using is unlikely to escape hard scrutiny in the ultra-wealthy family marketplace.

Conclusion

Advising ultra-wealthy families is a serious responsibility. After all, it is these iconic families who have driven American economic progress since the Industrial Revolution and who will continue to drive progress so long as free markets continue to exist. It's a challenging way to earn a living—extremely challenging, in fact—but also a delight. If you master the skills required to succeed in this enterprise, you will find the work to be gratifying and, if I might use the word, joyful. I wish you every success.

Bibliography

Alberts, I. (2018). *Passing the Torch: Preserving Family Wealth Beyond the Third Generation*. Hoboken, NJ: Wiley.

Bernstein, P. (1992). *Capital Ideas: The Improbable Origins of Wall Street*. New York: The Free Press.

Beyer, C. (2014). *Wealth Management Unwrapped: Unwrap What You Need to Know and Enjoy the Present*. New York: Rosetta Press.

Bogoricin, M., Pitters, C., & Gysi, D. (2018). *Family Offices and PIMCO: A Long-Term Partnership*. Newport Beach: Pacific Investment Management Company LLC.

Brest, P., & Harvey, H. (2018). *Money Well Spent: A Strategic Plan for Smart Philanthropy*. Palo Alto: Stanford Business Books.

Brunel, J. L. P. (2015). *Goals-Based Wealth Management: An Integrated and Practical Approach to Changing the Structure of Wealth Advisory Practices*. Hoboken, NJ: Wiley Finance.

Capgemini. (2019). *World Wealth Report*.

Castro, A., & Williams, R. (2017). *Bridging Generations: Transitioning Family Wealth and Values for a Sustainable Legacy*. Oviedo, FL: HigherLife Publishing.

Collier, C. (2006). *Wealth in Families*. Cambridge, MA: Harvard University Press.

Curtis, G. (2004). *Creative Capital: Managing Private Wealth in a Complex World*. New York: iUniverse Press.

Curtis, G. (2013). *The Stewardship of Wealth: Successful Private Wealth Management for Investors and Advisors*. Hoboken, NJ: Wiley.

Curtis, G. (2016). *Family Capital: Working with Wealthy Families to Manage Their Money Across Generations*. Hoboken, NJ: Wiley.

Deloitte. (2018). *Family Office Trends. Presentation to the Greycourt Advisory Council*. London: Deloitte Touche Tohmatsu Limited.

Domhoff, G. W. (n.d.). *Wealth, Income, and Power*. Retrieved from http://www1bpt.bridgeport.edu/~jconlin/EssayDomhoffWealthIncomePower.pdf

© The Author(s) 2020

121

G. Curtis, *Advising the Ultra-Wealthy*, https://doi.org/10.1007/978-3-030-57605-9

Ellis, C. (1992). *Classics II: Another Investor's Anthology*. Charlottesville, VA: Association for Investment Management and Research (now the CFA Institute).

Ellis, C. (1993). *Investment Policy: How to Win the Loser's Game*. Chicago, IL: Irwin Professional Publishing.

Evensky, H., Horan, H., & Robinson, T. (2011). *The New Wealth Management: The Financial Advisor's Guide to Managing and Investing Client Assets*. Hoboken, NJ: Wiley.

Foster, J. (2018). *The Right Portfolio: A Practical Exploration of Return, Risk, and Diversification, Investment Analysis* (pp. 70–492). Pittsburgh, PA: Carnegie Mellon University.

Freeman, D. (1991). *The Handbook on Private Foundations* (Revised Edition). Washington, DC: Council on Foundations.

Hauser, B. (2009). *International Family Governance: Avoiding Family Fights & Achieving World Peace*. Minneapolis, MI: Mesatop Press.

Hughes, J. (2009). *Family: The Compact Among Generations*. New York: Bloomberg Press.

Hughes, J. (2017). *Complete Family Wealth*. New York: Bloomberg Press.

Hughes, J., Massenzio, S., & Whitaker, K. (2013). *The Cycle of the Gift: Family Wealth and Wisdom*. Hoboken, NJ: Wiley.

Investment Management Consultants Association. (2014). *Certified Private Wealth Advisor: Candidate Body of Knowledge*. Greenwood Village, CO: IMCA Inc.

Jaffe, D. (2018). *Resilience of 100-Year Family Enterprises: How Opportunistic Innovation, Business Discipline, and a Culture of Stewardship Guide the Journey Across Generations*. North Charleston: CreateSpace Independent Publishing.

Jaffe, D. (2020). *Borrowed from Your Grandchildren: The Evolution of 100-Year Family Enterprises*. Hoboken, NJ: Wiley.

Khan, M., Serafeim, G., & Yoon, A. (2016). Corporate Sustainability: First Evidence on Materiality. *Accounting Review, 91*(6), 1697.

Kenyon-Rouvinez, D., & Park, J. (2020). Family Office Research Review. *The Journal of Wealth Management, 22*(4), 8–20.

Marston, R. (2014). *Investing for a Lifetime: Managing Wealth for the New Normal*. Hoboken, NJ: Wiley.

McCullough, T., & Whitaker, K. (2018). *Wealth of Wisdom: The Top 50 Questions Families Ask*. Hoboken, NJ: Wiley.

Nacht, J., & Greenleaf, G. (2018). *Family Champions and Champion Families: Developing Family Leaders to Sustain the Family Enterprise*. Chicago, IL: The Family Business Consulting Group, Inc.

Rosplock, K. (2014). *The Family Office Handbook: A Guide for Affluent Families and the Advisors Who Serve Them*. Hoboken, NJ: Wiley.

Santacruz, L. (2018). Wealth Management and Financial Advisory Services in the Asia-Pacific Region. *The Journal of Wealth Management, 21*, 3.

Schanzenbach, M., & Sitkoff, R. H. (2020). Reconciling Fiduciary Duty and Social Conscience: The Law and Economics of ESG Investing by a Trustee. *Stanford Law Review, 72*, 381.

Securities and Exchange Commission. (1998). *A Plain English Handbook*. Retrieved from https://www.sec.gov/pdf/handbook.pdf

Sheils, J. (2018). *The Family Board Meeting: You Have 18 Summers to Create Lasting Connections with Your Children*. Naples: 18 Summers Press.

Spiess-Knafl, W., & Scheck, B. (2017). *Impact Investing: Instruments, Mechanisms and Actors*. Cham, Switzerland: Palgrave Macmillan.

Swensen, D. (2000). *Pioneering Portfolio Management: An Unconventional Approach to Institutional Investment*. New York: Free Press.

Swensen, D. (2005). *Unconventional Success: A Fundamental Approach to Personal Investment*. New York: Free Press.

Zellweger, T. (2017). *Managing the Family Business: Theory and Practice*. Cheltenham: Edward Elgar Publishing.

UBS and PwC, *Riding the Storm, Billionaires Insights 2020*.

Index

© The Author(s) 2020
G. Curtis, *Advising the Ultra-Wealthy*, https://doi.org/10.1007/978-3-030-57605-9

9783030576042